These Splendored Isles

*Countless
the mountains
of Yamato,
and best of all
is Kagu,
the mountain
dropped from heaven.
Climbing,
I survey my realm:*

These Sple

*over wide plains
smoke wreaths hover,
across broad waters
seagulls fly;
O splendored land—
isles of the dragonfly—
my Yamato!*
—lines composed by
Emperor Jomei (629-41)
upon the occasion of
climbing Mount Kagu
and surveying the land
now called Japan; from
the *Manyoshu*

ndored Isles

The Scenic Beauty of Japan

photographs by Yoichi Midorikawa

introduction by Jiro Osaragi

text by Magoichi Kushida

guide by Michio Oi

foreword by William O. Douglas

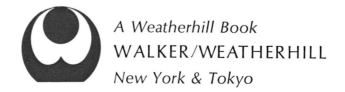

A Weatherhill Book
WALKER/WEATHERHILL
New York & Tokyo

Foreword   William O. Douglas

THE JAPANESE LOVE their lands, perhaps because they have so few acres. In spite of the burgeoning population and the anthills of Tokyo, Yokohama, and other metropolitan centers, there are quiet alcoves of great beauty across that green and well-watered land. And in recent years some twenty-three national parks have been created to provide sanctuaries for those who seek escape from the increasingly polluted zones of Japan's environment. Those parks, scattered throughout the Japanese islands, from the rugged coastlines and pounding surf of the north to the quiet beaches of the south, offer true wilderness retreats and provide the locales for most of the present photographs.

The title of the book, *These Splendored Isles*, reminds one of Shakespeare's "this sceptred isle," and, though the differences between England and Japan nature-wise are great, they have many similarities and share a great wealth of natural beauty. In this volume the beauties and natural wonders of Japan are brought to life with the eyes of Wordsworth by four famous contemporary Japanese.

The first is Yoichi Midorikawa (a surname with strong nature associations of its own, meaning "green river"), who has become Japan's greatest nature photographer. His specialty has won him numerous national awards in Japan.

Jiro Osaragi, who writes the introduction, is one of Japan's best-known contemporary novelists. Several of his works have been translated into English and published here.

Magoichi Kushida, who provides the texts for the photographs and has also selected the accompanying poems, is a well-known Japanese poet, essayist, and critic.

Michio Oi is an official of the Department of National Parks and a lecturer of note in landscaping, conservation, and park beautification. He has supplied a brief guide to the national parks of Japan and also an introduction to the Japanese national park system.

Together these four men have produced a delicate and sensitive account of Japanese nature under four headings—Color, Light and Shade, Form, and Movement and Stillness. And yet a further dimension is added to the book by a number of Japanese poets of many ages whose charming short verses accompany the photographs. Written in the traditional *haiku* and *tanka* forms for which Japanese poetry is noted, these constitute a short anthology of Japanese nature poetry and provide an insight into the Japanese love of nature.

In *Japan, a Short Cultural History*, Sir George Sansom writes of the pantheism that possessed Japan in the early centuries. That nature worship, he states, has as its mainspring not fear but "appreciation." The remote ancestors of modern Japanese ascribed divinity not only to the "powerful and awe-inspiring," such as the "sun and the moon and the tempest," and "to the useful, such as the well and the cooking pot," but also "to the lovely and pleasant, such as the rocks and streams, the trees and flowers." Their ancient religious rites had the purpose "to praise and thank as much as to placate and mollify their divinities."

In mythology their country was often known as the Land of Luxuriant Reed Plains, the Land of Fresh Rice Ears, the Land of Thousand Autumns. Their ancient gods had such names as the Princess Blossoming-Like-the-Flowers-of-the-Trees. Sansom says: "Even in these modern times a traveller off the beaten track can often see a tree or a rock by the wayside, adorned with the symbols of holiness, because it is of striking shape and therefore vaguely thought to harbor a divine presence."

Osaragi tells us how this ancient religion became the seedbed of an intense love of nature and a desire to conserve it. It is indeed the reason why the hills have long been forested and preserved, and even the mountains supervised with tender hands, why Japan is a country "with mountains that smile." Osaragi also gives us a poetic account of the seasons in Japan, their differences from those of Europe and North America, and, most important of all, the slow and subtle blending that takes place as one Japanese season gives way to the next.

Kushida tells us how many Japanese color words are now "syllabic renditions of English words," e.g., *rozu* for rose. Those who work in oil or watercolor use color to establish their themes. The color photographs of Midorikawa record the colors as they are, the reader giving them his own values. As Kushida observes, the present volume is a window "onto the colors of Japanese nature."

The light and shade of which Kushida speaks are largely unknown to urban man. Kushida writes of the impact of the sun and moon—on water and snow, on fields of grain, and on distant mountains. His story is for the outdoor man who may see in a few fleeting seconds as profound a transformation of nature as the apartment owner laboriously achieves with colors and lights in his month-long decorating project.

Kushida gives new perspective to the forms of nature; and he draws his examples both from islands in the seas and knife edges of cliffs and mountains. In each, man must act and react in conformity with the environment, accepting what "the world of nature lavishly offers." In the case of cliffs, where dizzy heights may make one ill or tempt one to suicide, the problem is to empty the mind of fear "so that the beauties of the world can refill it with singing happiness." A like adjustment must be made by one who walks the wildness unarmed; he must cast off fear and be at home with all the wild inhabitants he may encounter. The Japanese garden is a modified and manipulated form of this process and, as such, performs a valuable function. It is a "garden version of the world of nature," which is "fitted into a composition designed to calm the spirit."

Kushida tells somewhat the same story about movement and stillness—the air, clouds, rain, and tempests; the calm waters and the pounding seas; the hurricanes and thunderstorms. One finds beauty when he becomes part of the quiet or, as the case may be, the blustering process. The search for beauty leaves fear behind.

Oi's description of the location and nature of Japan's national parks provides an invaluable guide for the traveler.

Midorikawa's photographs are, as already noted, largely views of those national parks, for the simple reason that these areas contain some of the more celebrated scenery of a land justly noted for its landscapes. His notes on the photographs give them special meaning and show the reach of Japan from the zone of Havana, Cuba, to that of southern Canada.

This book has universal appeal because beauty has no barriers of race or nationality. This book has a special message because in all industrialized lands pollution of air and water and despoliation of the earth threaten the very existence of man himself. This book shows in moving eloquence the beauty of the good earth we are destroying.

Introduction   Jiro Osaragi

Land of Mountains and Waters

THE JAPANESE ARCHIPELAGO, lying east of the Asian continent, curves into the Pacific in a long, slender line running from twenty-five to forty-five degrees north. When the shores of Hokkaido are still locked in ice, the fields of Kyushu, the southernmost island, are blooming with pink cherries and yellow rape flowers. Ranges of mountains, like a backbone down its center, divide slender Honshu, the main island, into east and west sections. Warmed by the Pacific's Black Current, the eastern coast—called Front Japan—enjoys sunlight throughout the winter, whereas the villages and towns of Back Japan—the western side along the Sea of Japan— buffeted by blizzards, lie under a heavy load of snow. Even when the flowers of spring are blossoming in the east, in the west great silver sheets of snow glimmer on the mountaintops.

Pockets of flat land enclosed in narrow spaces between rugged peaks and the sea characterize Japanese topography. A passenger in an airplane flying along the coast is immediately struck by the number of rivers plummeting down steep courses among mountains and falling only short distances into the sea. The white riverbeds, which rise suddenly to great heights, look like staircases viewed from the bottom. No more than two or three of Japan's rivers flow calmly across wide expanses of land. Most of them enter the plains from narrow gorges and drop immediately to the sea. In most instances, their beds are dry until it rains, when they suddenly flood, only to become nearly parched again in a few days. Nonetheless, since mountain rainfall is heavy and melting snow plentiful, Japan is blessed with tremendous river power for the generation of electricity, and her coastal plains are amply irrigated.

An abundance of natural water sources has had a telling effect on the Japanese national spirit. For example, rice is the main crop, and paddies not only crowd the limited amount of flat lands, but also ascend the terraced hillsides and in some areas reach the very mountain peaks. Farmers have long been fond of watching the moon reflected in these shimmering sheets of black water in their paddies, called fields of a thousand layers.

The traditional Japanese house is so open to the natural elements that seasonal winds and rains become amiable companions of daily life. Unlike its Western counterpart, which tends to be a protective box with stingy window openings, the Japanese house promotes intimacy with the things of nature, and as a result, we Japanese have come to love water in all of its manifestations. We are equally pleased by the

11

pattering of rain and the reflections of flowers or willow branches in a stream's glassy surface. Both the noisy gurgling of a pebbly stream and the silent glide of a slender brook in a field of grass give us joy. So sensitive are we to waterfalls that we make distinctions between the large, grand ones, which we call males, and the gentler, smaller female ones. Roaring rapids and the lone fallen flower floating on a deep blue pool—both find room in the Japanese heart.

Our word for "landscape," derived from the Chinese, is made up of the characters for "mountain" and "water," and our ink paintings likewise often portray our homeland as a place of these same elements. In the conception of these pictures, water is so important an element that paintings of mountains without streams or lakes are considered poor things indeed. Even in the terrifying face of the yearly havoc wrought by typhoons and floods, the Japanese attitude toward water remains unchanged. National parks are always near some body of water, and indeed the very topography of the nation is such that water is always close at hand. Arid clouds and icy peaks alone are unsatisfactory to the Japanese spirit. Even Mount Fuji is thought more beautiful when seen reflected upside down in one of the five lakes at its base or in the waters of Tsuruga Bay. Our innate fondness for water probably explains the large number of photographs of bodies of water in this book.

The idea of a natural park as such is new to Japan. It springs, no doubt, from a sense of the importance of protecting natural beauty and of providing ample tourist areas as a countermeasure against the increasing incursions of modern urbanization. But even tourism is comparatively novel in Japan. Before the Meiji period and the days of the steam train and steamboat, most people disliked the idea of leaving their hometowns merely for the sake of pleasure trips. Though the destination might be within the confines of the Japanese nation, departing one's native province was tantamount to going to a foreign land. Japan was then divided among three hundred clans, each with its own boundaries and barrier stations and, in some cases, each with its own currency. Unless one went by palanquin, borne by human carriers, or rode horseback, all travel was by foot, no matter how distant the goal. Furthermore, the public peace was poorly maintained, and the roads were often unsafe. No wonder, then, that, except for official business or for the satisfaction of some especially ardent personal desire, most people preferred to remain at home. Aside from artists and the

very curious, no one went to distant places simply to enjoy the sights. Even should a person know of some splendid scenic wonder in another part of the country, in all likelihood there was no road to lead him there; consequently, the majority of the people stayed close to home, ending their days knowing only the beauty of their immediate surroundings.

Therefore, the Japanese, anchored all of their lives to one locality, developed a unique approach to the beauty of nature. Often seated day in and day out in front of a small garden, they learned to observe many subtle things in a single tree and to detect minute changes in the color of the sky, the shapes of clouds, or the textures of the grasses beside the path. This closely circumscribed field of vision also helped them develop the briefest, most concise poetic expression in the world, the *haiku,* which often deals with the changing of the seasons.

In Japan there are almost no expansive natural vistas of mountains and rivers. True, for many ages, the Japanese have been fond of selecting groups of famous views—the Views of Oe or the Eight Famous Views of Kanazawa—but Japanese choice is less scenic than human in mood. Now, of course, any remote, uninhabited backwoods is clearly visible from an airplane, and naturally the scale of our view of nature has altered correspondingly. Still, Japan clearly has nothing like the starry nights of the continenetal deserts, the icy peaks of the Alps, or the Norwegian fjords, the very tranquillity of which is overpowering.

Only on Hokkaido do virgin lands and primitive scenery remain. Here one may find ice-bound seas, glaciers, and the universal pristine awakening that is each spring. In Hokkaido forests, bears still roam, and lake waters preserve their original crystal clarity. But, even though the northern island has scenes comparable to cold continental ones, in the main Japan is an island of warmth. The waters of the Black Current and the Tsushima Current bathe her shores and produce an environment in which the mountains always wear thick coats of greenery and in which the seasons enact a delicately changing pageant. Japanese nature is calm, yet lively and ever changing. When the warmth of spring breathes over the land, the mountains smile, and we are infected with their joy. Perhaps people in other lands cannot understand the idea of mountains that smile.

England too is an island country, but there, when the dense, gray fogs of the long winter have fled and the brief spring is gone, in a swift moment it is suddenly summer. Japan lacks this kind of abrupt seasonal change. Here the alterations are gradual, 13 uneven, almost imperceptible. Barely conscious that he has said goodbye to spring, the Japanese may one morning find himself saying hello to summer. Nature changes her garments whimsically; the junctions between the seasons are gentle. In the dead of winter, we sometimes have balmy days—we call them little springs—and then again a cruel cold will often threaten spring flowers already in full bloom. Our seasons mix and combine, but of course we have some purely springlike days and some that are absolutely autumnal. Some Japanese are deeply convinced that winter is the most beautiful season of all.

Strangely poetic natural phenomena occur in Japan. In the vicinity of the city of Sendai, in the northeastern part of Honshu, on the brightest blue days sometimes winds drift down small snowflakes. We call them snow blossoms. Although the bamboo is considered a tropical plant, in this country it is not rare to find it heaped with snow, its branches bending, even breaking, under the load. This motif, a blend of frosty cold and tropical plant, is a favorite pattern for winter kimono cloth, and many classical poems compare unbearable love to the bamboo bending under the weight of snow, possibly because the lovestruck poet saw himself in the suffering plant. Such things do not occur in the tropical climes from which the bamboo comes. Such interminglings of infinitely subdivided seasonal change belong exclusively to Japan.

The blossoming of the cherries, beginning on the southern shores, gradually advances northward; the cherries of Hokkaido, in fact, flower one month later than those of Kyushu. Though they are not the rule, some nature lovers make the pilgrimage up the islands to follow the cherry in its flowery route. In autumn, the brocaded splendors of the scarlet maples perform similar feats, though in reverse direction. In their case, they are at the pinnacle of their loveliness first in the north and gradually redden later in the southern parts of the country. In the temperate middle regions, the autumnal crimson descends the mountainsides, as the trees on the higher and colder slopes turn to flame early to be followed by those farther down. It is not uncommon to hear people from the Hakone mountain area comment: "The maples here are not as nice as they will be, but if you go a a little higher up the mountain to the lakeside, they are truly splendid."

Even more fundamental, the mountains themselves greet us in totally different aspects when clothed in the colors of spring or autumn. Rivers do the same: the views of their banks vary according to the season. Even the sea is no exception. The autumn sea is so unlike that of spring that it seems impossible they are the same body of water. The very sun falls under the seasonal influence. On winter skiing trips to the snowbound north, I have encountered blindingly dazzling sunlight and almost purple skies. Perhaps as a result of the snow swathing the surroundings, on such days light seems richer and stronger than in midsummer. In a sense it reminds me of the whirling white solar discs of Van Gogh, though of course his was the sun of Arles, in the south of France. He is said to have wanted to visit Japan because of his infatuation with *ukiyoe;* how I would love to be able to show him our white winter suns and purple skies.

Though famous for its spring flowers, Japan is beautiful in winter too. Consider this scene: The sun is sinking behind the snowy mountains, only the tops of which are tinted rose. Their foothills are already in near night. The flatlands among the mountains are submerged in a watery, transparent air as green as emerald. Here and there red pinpoints of lights from farmhouses float into the darkness. The colors of the night deepen. Is this not a moment of supreme beauty?

Coasts facing the open ocean—such as Cape Shio on the Kishu Peninsula, Cape Ashizuri in Kochi, or the mountainous west coast of Sado Island, buffeted by Siberian cold—are rough and mighty, but the most truly Japanese in mood of all our coastlines are those of the Seto Inland Sea and the many islands dotting it. This is scenery unsuited to oil painting; it lends itself only to the gentle moods of the Oriental styles in which mists of gold soften and obscure outlines. Dissolving the barriers of time, Seto shows us today the same waters across which ships of envoys to the great T'ang dynasty passed or through which plowed the vessel of the Heian-period poet Ki no Tsurayuki on his return from a trip to Tosa, on southern Shikoku, that produced one of the most famous poetry-studded travel diaries in all Japanese literature. So undisturbed is the ancient calm of the sea that one would not be surprised to glimpse copper-skinned pirates sailing by, intent on raiding the capital and abducting lovely court ladies.

Although today oil refineries and industrial zones sprawl along the shore, modern excursion boats skim the waves, and passenger planes zoom overhead, in its elegance and beauty the Inland Sea still evokes tales of the medieval past. In this respect it resembles the green-watered Mediterranean and Aegean, where classical shepherds 15 seem yet to live on the islands and where one can almost catch the seductive sirens's songs. The Inland Sea is where a Japanese Daphnis and Chloe would live.

Here all is dreamlike. The islands float in tranquillity among hazes and mists. The countless pines of the shore, famous in song, echo sighs long dead, and the water, the element that pervades all Japanese scenery, rises in fine droplets into the air to cloud and soften shapes. It may have been because of the magic of these mists rising from the sea—I am not certain—but in my lifetime, I have seen two sunsets over the Inland Sea that were totally unlike anything I have experienced anywhere else. One of them occurred while I was traveling on a boat that, at the verge of evening, was just entering the Inland Sea. In Manila and in southern India along the Arabian Sea, I have witnessed flaming, passionately uni-colored red sunsets, but this was not that kind. As I watched the sky, it and its clouds gradually changed. Stately columnar clouds rose; whimsical cloudlets drifted by; and everything was bathed in a constantly mutating illumination of rose and pale green, shades that recall old paintings of the descent of the Buddha or of the Western Paradise. Watching that sunset, I could almost hear angelic music falling quietly on the waters. As the moving clouds changed shapes, their edges passed through five different colors. No unified fire, like the sunsets of India or the Philippines, this iridescence blossomed in the elegant semi-tones of the Heian period. If there is a paradise, it will be colored this way. There will be no primary colors. In the multicolored mirror of the waveless sea, Yagisa Island swayed gold and silver.

Opalescent sea sunsets can be found in many places in Japan, but on a separate occasion I saw quite another kind. Having gone to Cape Ashizuri on Shikoku and spent the night at Iyo-Osu, I crossed to Uno on the ferry and took a train home. We were following the shore of the Inland Sea, and just as we left Himeji and were at the place where Awaji Island comes into view, I observed a remarkable phenomenon. In the quickening blackness of the sky, the sun remained; it was as if someone had embroidered it on a dark background. Its colors were pale, yet brilliant—the fresh pink and white of a newly blossomed rose. The fragile half-colors of the clouds were of the kind typical of the Inland Sea and probably unique to Japan. An autumn evening was approaching. I took my eyes off the sky for a while, and when I looked again, layer upon layer of clouds on the dark western horizon looked like carpet dyed crimson with the blood of a lamb. Higher in the sky, they resembled great shelves incarnadined deep and vibrant, totally unlike the pale, radiant tones of the same sky only a few minutes before. These were colors I had never seen in a Japanese sky. Soon, however, night fell, and as my train entered the twinkling lights of Kobe, nothing relieved the sky's blackness but a thin slit of pale blue. The glory of the sunset had gone, but it remains indelible in my memory.

Thus has it been my good fortune to witness twice the hauntingly lovely sunsets of the Inland Sea. Perhaps the mists of the region produce them often.

Not only the seas, but the mountains as well alter subtly in this country. Whenever I go to Kyoto, I always visit the Sekisui-in of the temple Kozan-ji at Toga-no-o. Seated on the veranda, with the latticed doors swung up and open to reveal the view, I silently observe the mountains before me. I am especially fond of this place because of the effect created by the surrounding forest: the precisely aligned, rapidly growing trunks of the red pines and the foliage of the Kitayama cedars, stratified green clouds, seem to touch like layers of paper. Together they all but create a symphony. But once the mountain impressed me with a surprising depth. It was autumn, and the strong sunlight shot in rays among the trees and, falling on the ground, imparted a deep dimensionality to the surface of the mountain. Although I have long loved this view, on that day it seemed to greet me with a completely different face. No one was near; the short time in which I was able to sit among the sounds of a nearby river and confront my scene seemed to lengthen into an eternity. The ability to alter apparently magically is one of the most amazing aspects of Japanese water and mountains. Of course, it is only to be expected that on peaks towering three thousand feet, climatic conditions differ from morning to evening. Only in this country, however, do even humble hills transform their appearances in the twinkling of an eye.

Unlike continental mountains with bare backs hunched against the cold, almost all Japanese mountains are sun-bathed and clothed in rich forest. Our forefathers carefully forested and preserved the hills with great diligence, often for religious reasons since, in the Shinto faith, mountains, rivers, stones, and all other natural elements can be regarded as divine. Mount Miwa and the Three Mountains of Yamato, in Nara, as well as mounts Sugi and Akamatsu in Kyoto, have been carefully tended over the ages. In fact, almost all of the forests on Honshu receive careful attention of a kind probably unusual in the whole world.

A feature of Japanese scenery that I have not mentioned but that is, in its way, 17 almost as important as water is the large number of volcanoes on the islands. The most famous, Mount Fuji, is now extinct and its form fixed for all time; others, however, are still highly active—Sakurajima, Ago, and Mihara, to name only three. Their sharp peaks serenely touch the sky, and pastures and forests nestle at their feet, but by always threatening violence they interpolate dynamism into the normally placid scenery of the islands. They alone break from the ink-painting framework of tradition to enter a realm aesthetically akin to Western painting styles. Their activity is ceaseless. Within recent years, Mount Showa appeared like a raging giant in what had been a peaceful rice field, and even today it continues to rise and grow like bread dough in a pan.

Still it is not the presence of latent violence that is robbing Japanese scenery of its elegance. The cities men build are the culprits. Here, as in all other countries, nature has fled the soiled and arid urban environment. Exhaust fumes strangle people and plants alike, and crystal water, the once ubiquitous keynote of Japanese nature, is either polluted or nonexistent. The old castle moats are being filled to make highways, and towns with clean rivers are treasured rarities. Fortunately, however, national parks preserve something of the great stage on which nature performs its sometimes gentle, always awesome, drama of change. It is in this service to mankind that the true value of the parks lies.

The Scenic Beauty of Japan
photographs by Yoichi Midorikawa
text by Magoichi Kushida
and a short anthology of
Japanese nature poetry

A Note on the Poems

The poems that occasionally accompany the photographs are drawn from many different eras in the long history of Japanese literature. Taken together, they become a short but representative anthology of Japanese nature poetry. The selection was made principally by Magoichi Kushida, who is himself both a poet and a keen student of Japanese classical literature.

The translations are by Meredith Weatherby, with the assistance of Richard Gage, Miriam Yamaguchi, and Alexander Besher. The aim has been not so much word-for-word rendition as to recreate the spirit of the originals. Given the elliptical and often enigmatic nature of such verse, in a number of cases the translations are very free indeed, but without, it is hoped, violating the poets' essential intentions. Similarly, no effort has been made to reproduce the prosody of the originals, which are in the traditional forms of the five-line *tanka* and the three-line *haiku*.

The reader will quickly note that poems and photographs are often only vaguely related. Actually, instead of "matching," the two are intended to create a sort of antiphonal effect, the photographs showing specific scenes of Japan (described in the notes at the end of the book), while the poems describe different though equally specific scenes and moments and, in their totality, give something of the Japanese poet's reaction to nature in general.

20

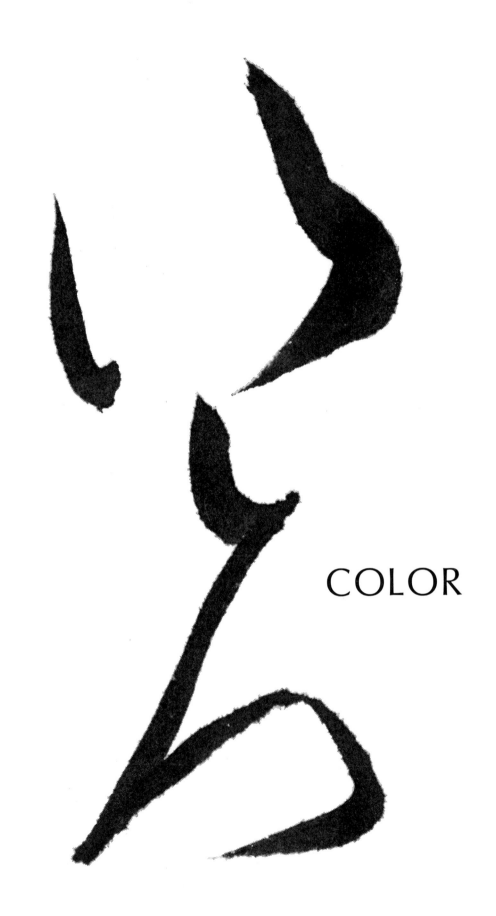

COLOR

How ELUSIVE A THING is color, how inextricably entangled with multitudes of associations and emotions, both personal and historical. And how difficult to define.

Why, for example, should Japan have been colored crimson on the maps used in my primary- and grammar-school geography classes? All the other nations of the world assumed much more moderate complexions: China a light yellow, the United States a somber green, England and her far-flung colonies pale pink, France lavender, and Germany subdued orange. Perhaps a patriotic cartographer selected fiery red in a futile attempt to make the limited Japanese land mass compare less unfavorably with its larger neighbors. Topographical maps put color to the practical uses of indicating elevations of mountains and depths of bodies of water. Looking at the matter thus, am I justified in assuming that colors in ordinary maps too play some kind of communicative role? If such is the case, I must scorn the foolish notion that perhaps Japan looks red when seen from the sky. It is within the realm of credulity, however, that the map designer chose scarlet because he considered it the favorite color of the Japanese people, but such a liberty would be to exceed the limits of his professional duty. Establishing a national attitude toward color is a problem of the utmost difficulty involving an analysis of a whole people's conception of color in general. Such an attitude always evades capture because it undergoes countless mutations through shifting ages and is always ensnared in the imperfections and vicissitudes of language.

When a child, I doted on a certain brand of chocolates filled with pink or pale green cream. In those days, we did not use plain words like "pink" or "green" to describe these confections. They bore much more evocative appellations. The pale pink was known by the name of the Japanese crested ibis and the light green by that of a certain gamefowl. Today not only are these words obsolete, but also the very birds have become so rare that they now enjoy governmental protection. The same is true in many instances in which color name and the plant or animal from which the name derived have become research topics for devotees of the recherché. Seated with a list of Japanese color names and a box of German pastels in front of me, I am struck with the impossibility of equating one with the other.

But the problem of assigning color names is by no means new. I have read of a certain priest in the distant past who once wrote about the difficulty of giving a name to the peculiar color of freshly budded pampas grass. Enjoying a view of a field of the plant from the hill on which he stood, he wanted to convey the thrill of its beauty in accurate terms, but he was ultimately reduced to a choice between two words. Both were similar; there was no more than a slight—though significant—semantic shade between them. But the choice proved impossible. I myself, stading on a similar hill overlooking a field of young pampas, have experienced the same dilemma; and I therefore feel a profound kinship with the priest and his color quandary. Nevertheless, I live in the modern world, and like most other aspects of my being, my sense of color is conditioned by contemporary surroundings.

Perhaps the Japanese of today have not lost their color sensitivity, but it differs sharply from that of the people of the past. This is only to be expected since, in our bustling world, no one has the leisure carefully to examine, criticize, and select even works of art, let alone the colors of objects of daily use. On the other hand, this apparently unfortunate situation results in an open acceptance of color ideally suited to appreciation of the wonders of nature, where excess ratiocination and theorizing hamper the ability to enter directly into the profundity of natural beauty. Sadly enough, however, the modern urban dweller has all too few opporunities to come into contact with this beauty. Often convinced that a little nature is worse than none at all, the city worker ignores even the scant green of the trees along the streets, he considers the few flowers blooming in the public parks beneath consideration, and he hurries to his hermetically sealed office to work all day by artificial illumination because he is persuaded that the city has no sky worthy of mention.

Nevertheless, this sad man has not entirely forgotten nature. Sometimes, in reaction to the blandishments and alluring nonsense about sunlight, ozone, and greenery pumped forth by travel agencies, he ventures out for a weekend in the country. But while there he makes surprising demands. The mountain climber atop a breathtaking peak pines for a television set, or the visitor to the seaside complains of the lack of a swimming pool. Confronted with attitudes of this kind, one wonders whether modern man has forgotten the unalloyed joys of nature or whether perhaps he ever knew about them at all. Fortunately, however, not everyone is this blind. Some people continue to ache for the loveliness of the mountains and fields, but the problem of color, even for them, is a thorny one. What is the best approach to it?

The painter, amateur or professional, is both sensitive to and demanding of gradations and variations in color. He knows that the tones and combinations required to reproduce faithfully the greens and browns of the highlands are endless, but his approach is ill suited to the true nature lover for a single cogent reason: his intentions are different. Trained through long years of discipline, the artist seeks to impose his own theories, ideas, or emotions upon the lines, forms, and colors of nature. His is not the business of realistic re-creation of what can be seen with the objective eye. He does not accept the colors of nature; he strives to use them to his own ends.

If art, then, fails to help in the search for an approach to color, will history be more congenial? Here again, disappointingly, the ground is shaky. First, attempting to call from oblivion the emotions of people long vanished involves tremendous subjective interpretation. But perhaps more important, we must remember that the attitudes of the people of the past toward natural scenery were conditioned by physical limitations virtually unknown to modern man. For our forefathers, distant mountains were an almost inaccessible, but beautiful, backdrop, often all the more effective for being swathed in concealing mists. These people did not scale towering peaks or plumb valley depths, but in their literature they recorded an aspect of their poetic feeling for nature that conveys powerfully even to us. They so tenderly loved the delicate pink of the spring cherry and the noble green and red of pine and maple that among their chief joys were convivial—often inebriating—outings to glory in the beauty around them. Today, we arrange similar excursions, but for us conviviality overshadows aesthetic joy. Our souls no longer echo to the blush of the blossom or the flame of the leaf.

Our eye for color has changed; perhaps in response, nature has rearranged her color schemes. Today we prize the russets and browns of the fields more than the crimson and green of valleys filled with maple and pine; and instead of thrilling to the serenity of a pure blue sky we find joy in the swirling of gray, storm-wracked clouds. It may be, however, that these are acquired tastes.

Westernization is one of the aspects of our eclectic culture that has changed our attitude toward color. Although the Japanese blend of East and West is by and large skillful, it has had some peculiar results. I, for instance, though by no means infatuated categorically with all Occidental things, frequently seek among the beauties of the Japanese countryside similarities to famous European views. The prevailing influence of the West in daily life in this country has changed the eye with which I see things or at least has cast a different tint on the lens of that eye. Once watching the fleeting pale green of the evening sky just as the sun was almost out of sight, I thought, "How like the flesh of an apple that color is." Imagine my surprise when I later discovered that, in fact, "apple green," or *appuru gureenu* as we say it, is the fashionable name for the color. Indeed, almost all of our color words are now syllabic renditions of English words—*orenji* (orange), *buamiriyon* (vermilion), *rozu* (rose), and so on. I have nearly come to the conclusion that, without my being aware, all the colors of the natural world have put on foreign airs.

Abstracting color from its maze of associations and attempting to treat it as an independent entity is impossible. Furthermore, in nature, color only assumes its full meaning in conjunction with light, form, and movement. Even when these are all considered together, however, it is difficult to pin color down for a close examination. Nevertheless, if the heart of the viewer is open to the grandeur of what he sees, he will abandon intellectual requirements; he will simply observe and understand.

Once on a visit to a mountainous district I talked with an old woman who told me an interesting story. She said that a young relative had recently cut a window in the wall of her kitchen to provide needed extra light. From that window, she enjoyed a view of the colorful changing pageant of the mountains across the valley from her house. For years she had lived near them, but never before had she known their true beauty in the panoply and splendor of the procession of seasons. Never before, that is, until someone made a window for her.

This is the gift the following pages offer us—windows onto the colors of Japanese nature. We need not stop to name the colors, neither in Japanese nor in English: they are here, waiting to move into our blood.

PHOTOGRAPHS

1. Kegon Falls Through Blossoms, Nikko
2. Wild Rhododendron, Nikko
3. Fallen Leaves on Lake Chuzenji, Nikko
4. "Coral Grass" at Lake Notoro,
            Abashiri Regional Park
5. Blossoms of "Boulder Plum," Daisetsu
6. Lilies of the Valley at Lake Notoro,
            Abashiri Regional Park
7. Spring at Iwaobetsu, Shiretoko
8. Autumn Colors at Goshiki Marsh,
            Bandai-Asahi
9–10. Autumn at Mount Mikura,
            Towada-Hachimantai
11. Highland Autumn, Bandai-Asahi
12. Primeval Autumn, Towada-Hachimantai
13. Golden Leaves on Tsuta Marsh,
            Towada-Hachimantai
14. Otaki Falls, Towada-Hachimantai
15. Water Reflections at Cape Okama,
            Rikuchu Coast
16. Spring Snow in Daikoku Forest,
            Towada-Hachimantai

17. Oze Lilies, Nikko
18. Red Berries at Yunoko Lake, Nikko
19. Ezo Reeds, Nikko
20. Pampas Fields of Sengokubara,
            Fuji-Hakone-Izu
21. Gilded Autumn at Yunoko Lake, Nikko
22. Red Fuji, Fuji-Hakone-Izu
23. New Autumn Snow on Mount Daisen,
            Daisen-Oki
24. Peaks at Dawn, Chubu Mountains
25. White Birches in Autumn Foliage,
            Joshinetsu Heights
26. Alpine Flowers, Chubu Mountains
27. Autumn Seascape, Sanin Coast
28. Spring Hillside, Seto Inland Sea
29. Peach Blossoms, Seto Inland Sea
30. Chrysanthemums, Seto Inland Sea
31. Sunset over Islands, Seto Inland Sea
32. Wild Rhododendron, Aso
33. Sea Grotto of Nanatsu-gama,
            Genkai Regional Park
34. Kishuku Village, Saikai

The green hills,
the blue mountains—
these, and my grateful eyes.
                    —Ho-o

My mantle wet
by gentle rains of spring—
how green the color of the fields!
                    —Ki no Tsurayuki

Spring has stolen quietly
into the sky:
mists drift about the heavenly Mount Kagu.
                    —Empress Jito

A village of a hundred houses,
and not one gate
without chrysanthemums.
                    —Buson

2

3

4

Only a flowering grass,
but when I learned its name,
I looked again.
			—Teiji

The moonflower dons
a gleaming robe of morning dew—
and fades away.
			—anonymous, from the *Kokinshu*

How strange! Using only white, frost has dyed the autumn leaves a thousand different hues.
—Toshiyuki no Asaomi

12

An autumn wind—and a dog barking at the sound of leaves.

—Sono

Departing, autumn scatters maple leaves along the way.

—Otsuyu

Going out to see, I found spring caught in my willow.
　　　　　　　　　　　　　　　　—Chodo

18

Only Mount Fuji remains unburied above spring's fresh green.
　　　　　　　　　　　　　　　　—Buson

*Flood tide beneath
a rising moon,
and the young reeds
of Naniwa Bay
awash in whitecaps.*
　　　—Fujiwara no Hideto

*An autumn moor—
and a single bird
to keep me company.*
　　　—Senna

22

24

In the depths of the autumn sky I found—myself.

—Seisei

25

26

Preparations for spring are all but done—
moon and plum blossoms.
                                    —Basho

See the capital in spring brocade, a weaving
of cherry blossoms and budding willows.
                                    —Sosei

29

30

32

Bending low, a branch of redbud has pierced the fence.

—Buson

A single morning glory! The color of a deep, deep pool!

—Buson

The fishermen's nets—are they not stained blue by the summer sea?
                                                                    —Fusei

LIGHT
AND SHADE

WHY ANALYZE the prismatic reds, greens, and blues lavished on the air by water drops sparked with rays of light? The scientifically oriented mind knows that the colors are caused by light's passing from a medium of lesser to one of greater density, but the knowledge in no way increases or diminishes the naked beauty of the phenomenon. Just as minute, particularized examinations of each element in a glorious natural panorama reduce the whole to less than the sum of its parts, so scientific analysis, though certainly meaningful in its way, robs light of its many-faceted splendor. My purpose is to point out some of light's wonder-working effects on a large scope. Therefore, I will not train powerful binoculars on the individual blades of grass on a hillside. Instead I want to reveal the whole picture and the variations light's many manifestations work on it. I want consider the miracles light and shade create in nature.

As the source of all human vision, light has been appropriated by man as something specially his own, at time a source of excess happiness, at others an object of calumny. Nevertheless, light bathing a scene floods each flower, tree, bird, and butterfly with a kind of ecstasy. The oppressed forget their chains, and the weary and wounded revive under the healing balm of light's embrace. In other words, light is a magician capable of converting the earthly into the ethereal.

Once lost in a blizzard, I crouched in the shelter of a tree until the snow stopped falling. Just before dawn, the clean-scoured sky unfurled a paling, but still star-glittering, canopy over the world. Looking for my no-longer-visible tracks of the previous night, I walked out from the friendly shelter of the tree. The only evidence of my existence was the footprints I was making at the moment. At length, I came upon an open riverbed, where snow, drifting down the steep banks on either side, had mounded deep, white, and so firm that my feet barely dented it. Gusts whirled small cyclones of snow dust as I took my initial steps on the crunching surface. Then, suddenly, morning's first rays, slipping down the mountainside, miraculously transformed the white riverbed into a sheet of dazzling colors. It was as if the prime touch of morning light awakened in the perfect, gemlike snowflakes fleeting memories of the glories of the sky-home from which they had fallen. But even as I stood in awe of this wordless hymn to beauty, the sun rose higher, extinguishing the jewel-colored fires and leaving behind only a brilliant sheet of white. What had worked this miracle in the dead of winter in a valley where no wind sighed, where no birds called, where not even the track of a solitary hare marred the perfection of the snow? The everyday wonder of morning light.

Light's beauty, however, is not always of this sudden, dramatic kind. We are often intoxicated by the gentle light that sinks slowly among the shady fissures of great boulders or by the mystery of glimmering light filtering through water and dancing on the surfaces of submerged objects. Such loveliness transcends wonder and pleasure; it is an instantaneous revelation demanding more than admiration. So too is the milky light of the moon, source of more mystic legend and greater hope of profound encounters than her effulgent brother the flaming sun. Still it is the light of the great sun that, when reflected on bodies of water, undergoes protean changes of mood and rhythm much like those of musical composition.

I recall a bright, calm day when I stood by the shore of a lake in which the sky, the opposite bank, its trees, and the mountains retreating in stately file were reflected as perfectly as in a mirror. A cameraman has set up his tripod by the lake and was engrossed in composing a photographic résumé of what his eyes saw. Wanting to speak but fearful of disturbing him with the banalities of ordinary introductions, I simply commented that, even should he take his picture upside down, the flawless reflection would produce precisely the same effect as the scene of which it was the mere ghost. The cameraman answered me with a cheery laugh and went about his work. In only an hour, however, a sudden wind had shattered the lake-mirror into thousands of gray wavelets, each fracturing the ball of the reflected sun into countless divergent flashings. Gone was the placid perfection of the lake surface, and in its place danced a spangled expanse of leaden waters. The cameraman, having changed film and lenses, was now busily attempting to capture the mood of the new light. Respecting his endeavor, I left him in peace.

Dramatic lighting, calm gentle illumination, and the washing floods of light that cast perfect images on water are not all of light's moods. In fact, perhaps its most important role in scenic appreciation is the creation of contrast and accent that results from the slanting sunlight of morning or evening when colors and shadows deepen. Light's secret is rich variety. One may introduce a certain amount of color into a drab life by hanging pictures or by rearranging old or purchasing new furniture. Such willful alterations in a natural scene are, of course, out of the question. We cannot change the mountains or move a lake to suit our aesthetic sensibilities or to satisfy our craving for variety. But miraculous light, given time, can work the wonder of change for us. Under the effects of subtle illumination, even intrinsically uninteresting scenery assumes new charm and often manifests heretofore unperceived possibilities of human appeal.

But, again, I must not intrude overlong on the cameraman as he records so splendidly the many miracles of light—and its complement, shade.

PHOTOGRAPHS

35. Frozen Sea, Shiretoko

36. Broken Ice Floes, Shiretoko

37. Forest Lake, Akan

38. Lake Mashu, Akan

39. Snow on Tokachi Mountains, Daisetsuzan

40. Swirling Snow in Tokachi Mountains,
        Daisetsuzan

41. Snow-clad Trees at Hakkoda,
        Towada-Hachimantai

42. Mountain Rapids at Oirase,
        Towada-Hachimantai

43. Reflections in Akanuma Marsh,
        Towada-Hachimantai

44. Autumn Light at Oirase,
        Towada-Hachimantai

45. Twilight over Oze Marsh, Nikko

46. Pastureland at Dusk, Joshinetsu Heights

47. Rainbow at Kegon Falls, Nikko

48. Mountain House, Hakusan

49. Lighthouse, Hinomisaki Cape

50. Pearl Rafts, Ise-Shima

51. Mushima Lighthouse, Seto Inland Sea

52. Shionomisaki Reef by Day,
        Yoshino-Kumano

53. Shionomisaki Reef by Night,
        Yoshino-Kumano

54. Lightning over the Bisan Seto,
        Seto Inland Sea

55. Island of Mizushima-nada, Seto Inland Sea

56. Sea with Boats, Seto Inland Sea

57. Islets of Southern Kujukuto, Saikai

58. Waves of Mountains, Saikai

59. Silver Sea at Cape Muroto,
        Muroto-Anan Coast Regional Park

60. Outside Tomioka Bay, Unzen-Amakusa

61. Hyuga Seascape,
        Nichinan Coast Regional Park

62. Amakusa Seascape, Unzen-Amakusa

63. Hamlet at Takachiko, Kirishima-Yaku

64. Mount Kaimon by Night, Kirishima-Yaku

65. Coral Shallows, Okinoerabu Island

66. Ripples over Coral, Okinoerabu Island

75

The dawn sky is veiled with mist
like the spring-colored smoke
from Mount Fuji,
from the fields of heaven.
                    —Jion

The cold wind . . . the falling leaves . . .
and night by night
more moonlight floods my garden.
                    —Takeko

A field of golden flowers:
to the west, the setting sun;
to the east, the rising moon.
                    —Buson

A cool summer night,
with the moon
sleeping in water.
                    —Ryusui

By dawn, even the storm lies buried in snow.

—Shiro

Soaring skylarks— treading the clouds, dining on mist.

—Shiki

The winter storm has blown the setting sun into the sea.
                                        —Soseki

39

40

The winter moon, abandoned in a field, friendless.
                                        —Roseki

Flying fish—leftover moonlight?
　　　　　—Basho

The Mogami River—
how swifty it washes away
the summer!
—Shiki

Dead leaf piles on dead leaf; rain beats on rain.
—Kyodai

45

In the autumn twilight, one solitary crow perched on a bare branch.
                                        —Basho

Opening the window, I showed the priest an autumn rainbow.
                                        —Meisetsu

46

49

While the setting sun casts shadows
through my brushwood gate,
can it be raining in the mountains over there?
                    —Seisuke

Under a sky clear and still, moonlight frozen in water.
—anonymous, from the *Kokinshu*

While I slept, tattered wisps of clouds have formed a mountain.
—Issa

Lightning!—and suddenly there flashes the face of the sea.

—Basho

54

55

In the dawning sky,
the spring-colored smoke
of Mount Fuji,
the hovering mist . . .
                    —Jien

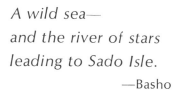

A wild sea—
and the river of stars
leading to Sado Isle.
                    —Basho

Two young bamboos
holding the autumn moon
between them.
                    —Shiei

The spring sea—ripples of light the whole day long.
                                                    —Buson

FORM

ONCE, AFTER CLIMBING a long, steep road and arriving at last at a pass, I stood for a while contemplating the splendid view of the distant mountains that were actually the goal of my ascent. No, in fact, contemplating is not what I did. I really indulged in various fancies about the view and finally formulated one interpretation that I considered definitive. Why imagine things about a view? And what should one do if fancies conflict with realities? There is no need to worry about this. The pleasures of the imagination and the joys of contact with actual scenes are different. No conflict can exist between them, and it is easy to turn immediately from one to the other. Although formerly, when sated with travel, I longed to shut away scenic treasures in the flask of my memory, for some reason that tendency has been less pronounced in recent years. All natural beauty thrills me, and when I hear someone say that his wonder at the spacious grandeur of scenery in other lands has robbed the beauty of Japan of all stimulation for him, I think how sorrowful he must be.

But to return to the view I enjoyed from the mountain pass, it was new to me. This was my first visit to this place. Before me marched ranks of mountains cut by a valley as deep as the one I had just left. Here and there the hills concealing the valley looked like the folds of the bottom of a kimono skirt. In the distance glittered a river wending its way through a plain, and still farther beyond and partly veiled in mists ranged the noble mountain peaks. The angle of the sun bathing the slopes in purple-gray was such that the ordinarily visible foothills were completely obscured.

I was uanble to cope mentally with the whole connected series, but I had no trouble recalling the names of individual peaks; and as I did so, memories of long-gone days rose fresh in my mind.

Some people, content with geometry and objectivity, describe mountains as pointed, like the teeth of a saw, or rounded, like the head of an elephant, and let the matter drop at that. I, however, insist on memory and evocation of associations. Eyes grown dim with age no longer see the boulders and trees on the mountainsides, but the eye of memory recalls even more subtle details. When I sketch the line of a range of mountains it is not with the intention of producing a picture, but with the hope of mentally capturing the mountains's form so that later I may describe it in words. Images flash before the eyes; like clouds they are born we know not where, they drift by and vanish. But the images stored in the memory eternally color the way we see all things.

To my mind's eye, an island is the top of a mountain cut off horizontally by surrounding waters. Similarly, a mountain in a mist becomes an island in a white sea. The submerged part of an island is invisible; mist-veiled mountainsides too are hidden from sight. But mists disperse, whereas waves forever isolate islands in watery confinement. Those waters, though scientifically fathomable, confound the soul with the mystery of the unknowable. Sometimes raging waves, crashing against cliffs, forbid approach to islands. Only a miracle could bring one safe to an island shore in such a storm, but is this not the true value of an island? And does that value not increase as the island becomes more inaccessible?

Sometimes I dream of a round island I once saw from the window of an airplane. Like all islands, it was isolated and thus, in a sense, a prison, a place of exile. But by the same token, if isolation from the world is desirable, an island can also be a paradise. To test this idea, I longed to live on an island. I wanted to visit the round one I saw from the airplane to discover what kind of life would be possible for me there. Perhaps island scenery is more interesting, even on a small scale, when enriched by inlets and promontories, but the very perfection of the roundness of this island captured my imagination. Several years later, a small motorboat took me there, and my curiosity was satisfied.

A different kind of island once fascinated me by its rocky, isolated, impregnable shoreline, which unforgettably repelled approach. In spite of its forbidding aspect, however, I wanted to entrust myself to it, to leave something of myself there.

Once a famous priest named Myokei, who had visited a certain island, upon returning to his home, penned a lengthy letter and entrusted it to a messenger to deliver to the island. Not unreasonably, the messenger asked to whom the letter should be delivered. Myokei replied that he was to take it to the island of Karima and, after announcing loudly that it was from the priest Uemo Myokei, simply throw it on the ground and return. Perhaps in this way Myokei thought to leave something of his heart on the island, though he could not be there in person. Thus the very idea of an island in its isolation inspires the heart with the romance of a way of life mysteriously unknown because cut off from the commonplace.

From the dimmest recesses of time, a war has raged between land and sea. Islands are one manifestation of the battle. Cliffs are another. And it is on the dizzying edge of the wind- and sea-hacked precipice that the forms of nature assume their most 113 overwhelming aspect. Here, where yawning vastness seems to swirl upward and to drag one from his precarious perch, there is no security. Neither the deep-rooted tree, whose branch could provide safety if one would but trust it, nor the solid boulder under one's feet can calm the alarms of the soul. Under these awesome circumstances, Man must do something himself. He must adopt some course of conformity with the environment and, by thus making his own pronouncement, free himself to enjoy the beauty around him. This pronouncement may take the simplest form of merely sitting down and, by lowering the eye level, dispelling the fear of falling. Or it may lead the man to pick his way down the sheer face of the inhospitable cliff till, standing on the beach below, he can associate himself intimately with the natural world without suffering agonies of physical danger. Either approach is correct because both liberate the spirit from fear and thereby open it and empty it so that the beauties of the world can refill it with singing happiness.

In the final analysis, the mind must be ready to accept what the world of nature lavishly offers, but this does not mean that a certain amount of tampering with natural forms is wrong. For instance, the Japanese garden is a perfect example of adjusting Nature to serve a soul-calming and satisfying purpose. "Why," one might ask, "should a rural family, occupying a house set in the midst of scenery of great natural beauty, deliberately wall off a small patch of ground and create in it an artificial and closely regulated version of the natural world?" The reason is a complex one, somewhat clarified, however, by the relationship of such a garden to the other elements of the farmhouse and its layout.

The visitor to a typical Japanese farm first crosses a courtyard rich with the smells of compost and chicken coops. After entering the earthen-floored entrance room, where he removes his shoes, he passes through the cool depths of the family room, the smoke-blackened beams of which cross high over the hearth set low in the floor. Moving still deeper into the house, he comes at last to a formal sitting room, used only for the reception of guests. On the outer side of the room is a small veranda beyond which is the garden. The gravel has been freshly raked, all dead leaves removed, and perhaps the trees newly pruned in honor of the visitor. Beyond the garden may be a splendid view of a nearby mountain or forest, but this is excluded. The garden version of the world of nature has been carefully domesticated to suit the scale of the vase of flowers or the hanging picture scroll ornamenting the alcove inside the room. This is not the raw, thrilling nature of island or cliff. It is a humanized version of one or perhaps many natural forms. But these forms are fitted into a composition designed to calm the spirit; this, too, is a valid approach.

Another valid, even miraculous, approach is in the pages that follow. Sitting quiet and secure in our own living rooms, we see with the photographer some of the stupendous forms of Japanese nature, he shows us the way, we are there with him.

PHOTOGRAPHS

67. Cliffs on Saga Island, Saikai

68. Snow on Shiretoko Mountains, Shiretoko

69. Ice Floes, Shiretoko

70. Early Spring in Hachiman Marsh,
                        Towada-Hachimantai

71. Hot Spring at Goshogake,
                        Towada-Hachimantai

72. Kitayamasaki Shoreline, Rikuchu Coast

73. Natural Tunnels, Rikuchu Coast

74. Mountains on Mountains,
                        Towada-Hachimantai

75. Snow Slope, Towada-Hachimantai

76. Dead Trees in Snow, Joshinetsu Heights

77. Snow Panorama at Kasagadake,
                        Joshinetsu Heights

78. Snowscape at Mount Gozen, Hakusan

79. Snowy Grove, Joshinetsu Heights

80. Winter at Sengatake Falls, Chichibu-Tama

81. Hamasaka Dunes, Sanin Coast

82. Dunes and Snow, Sanin Coast

83. Islands at Bisan Seto, Seto Inland Sea

84–87. Beach Patterns, Seto Inland Sea

88. Stone Quarry, Seto Inland Sea

89. Field of Eroded Limestone,
                        Akiyoshidai Regional Park

90. Sea-carved Rock,
                        Nichinan Coast Regional Park

91. Stairstep Wheat Field, Seto Inland Sea

92. Fishing Fleet, Seto Inland Sea

93. Beech Trees in Snow, Daisen-Oki

94. Natural Bridge at Kuniga, Daisen-Oki

95. Dead Coral, Okinoerabu Island

As for spring . . .
seen till yesterday
among the waves,
now veiled in mist—
mountains of Awaji.
                    —Shunkei

Winter moon!
How sharp the outlines
of Sawtooth Rock!
                    —Buson

Gently wander
the streams
through fields of spring.
                    —Buson

Looking at the lotus,
can one imagine
any other flower?
                    —Shunsui

68

69

71

The rising moon paints a pine tree on the blue of the sky.
—Ransetsu

Beneath the harvest moon my shadow sees me home.
—Sodo

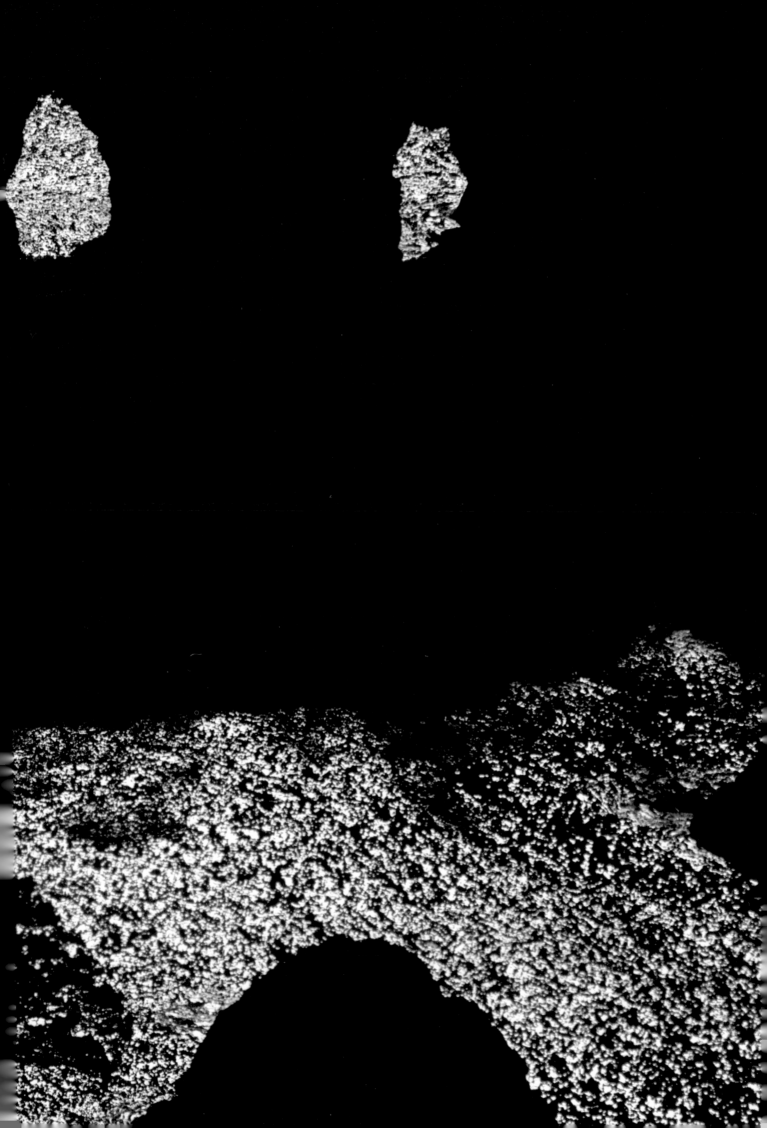

75

76

77

78

The snow has captured
both field and mountain—
nothing remains.

—Joso

You have gone, and no flowers remain upon this earth.
　　　　　　　　　　　　　　　　　　—Soseki

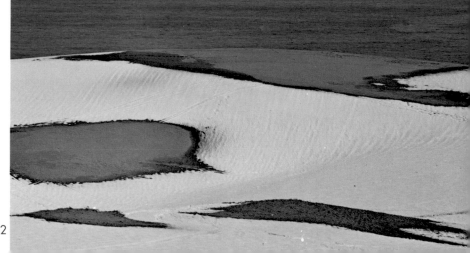

*Wisps of mist over the sea of Nago, and far in the offing
white waves breaking over the setting sun.*
—Fujiwara no Sanesada

The stillness! Voices of cicadas pierce the very rocks.
                                                    —Basho

85

86

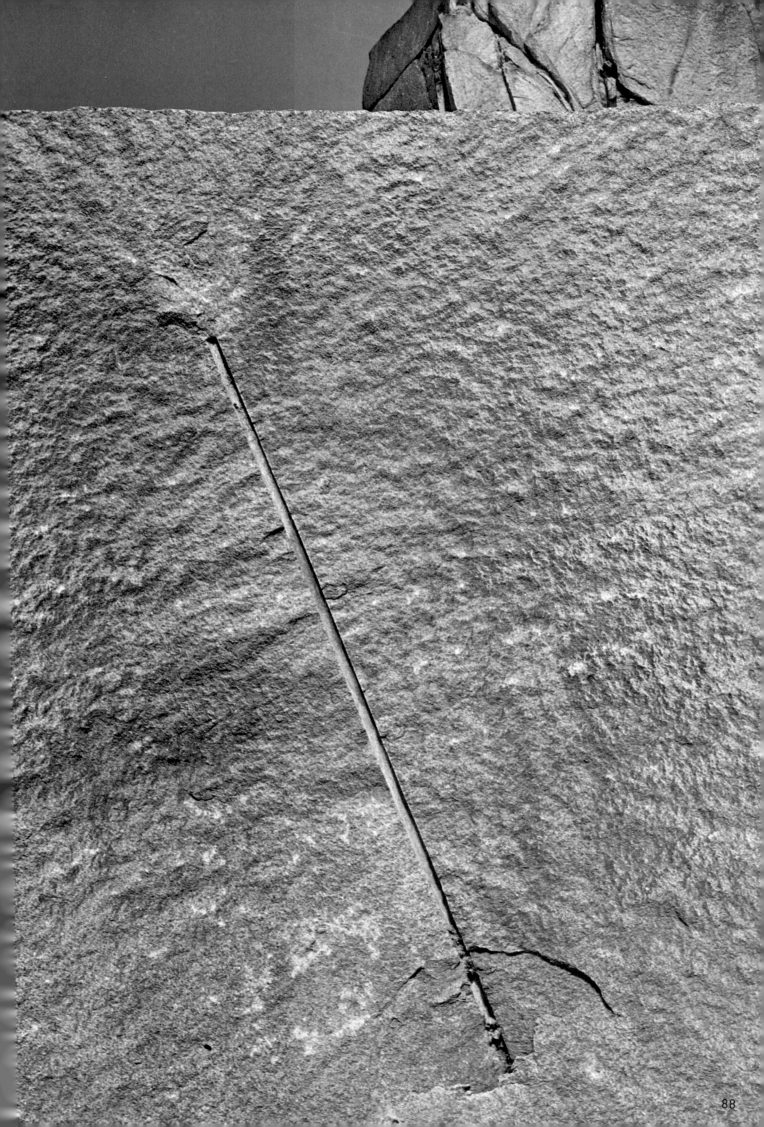

A cold night—and the sound of waterfalls crashing to the sea.
                                                        —Kyokusui

Invisible the shape
of spring's arrival—
but, see, the ancient willows
along the river bank.
          —Prince Sukehito

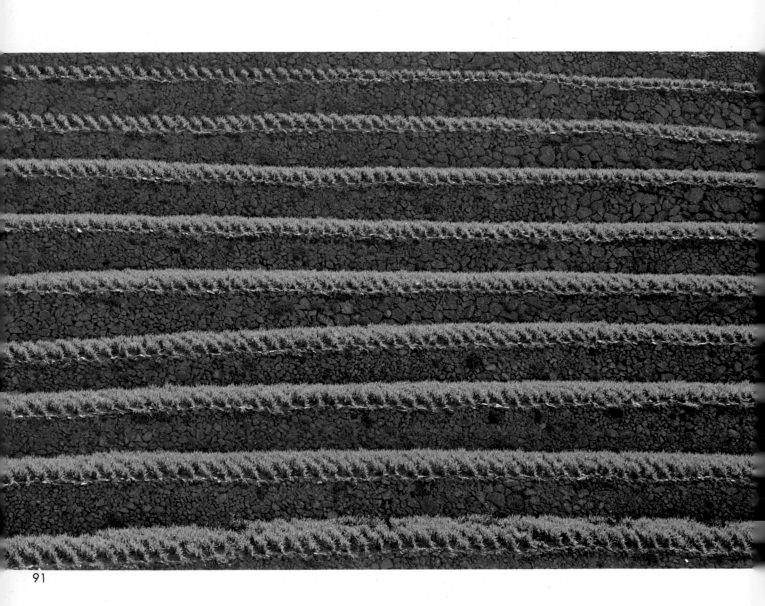

Our horses abreast, we hurry onward:
already are they falling like the snow,
the cherry blossoms of home?
        —anonymous, from the *Kokinshu*

In the spring rain
even the sturdy pines
are sleeping.
        —Torin

The year's first snow—
just enough to gently bend
the leaves of daffodils.
        —Basho

94

95

A summer beach—and the calligraphy of seashells.
                                        —Senrian

MOVEMENT
AND STILLNESS

THE STATELY SWEEP of clouds, the lashing of the storm, the lapping of the waves, and the howling of the wind all reverberate in the human soul. Our role is to receive them all unquestioningly and to allow them to play upon us as if we were instruments carefully tuned to their music.

Some clouds seem to flow, whereas others, we say, float. We describe them and give them names according to the associations they awaken in our minds. Often the weather subsequent to appearances of certain kinds of clouds influences our selection of appellation. For example, "woolpack" describes the clouds' fleecy appearance, but "rainball" suggests an unfortunate turn in the weather.

Travelers anxiously scan the sky for signs of clouds that might spoil their pleasures. They rejoice in undisturbed blue for purely practical reasons. But the lover of nature, though moved by a clear October day, sometimes longs for clouds to add profundity to the scene. His wish is not pure human selfishness flung in the face of nature. It is instead a reflection of the artistic knowledge that perfection is at times vapid and that the flaw frequently is the agent that binds the elements of a composition in true harmony.

My own love of clouds springs from a fondness for fancy. Just as I delight in observing moving clouds as they alter a scene, so I find pleasure in imagining what a photographed valley would be like if its greenery were changed to crimson and amber or if the clouds above it assumed different shapes. Wondering what a picture would be like if it were transformed from summer to autumn or what transformations dancing winter snows would work on it is my way of giving mental action to the physically static.

Once I visited a beach on the eve of an impending storm. Although the wind was not yet strong, intermittent squalls lashed the shore, and the churning sea was already made turbid by thick mud poured into it from a nearby river. As I stood on a sandbank, carved perhaps by the waves or perhaps by winds that had blown wild a few days before, I watched the sea crumble great chunks from my pedestal, and I realized that soon there would be nothing left of it. Behind me a hill that should have been clearly visible was obscured by driving sheets of fine rain. The day was ill-omened, and my spirits mutely wept in sympathy.

On another day, however, I stood on another beach where sand, sea, and wind, wearing more benign countenances, wrapped my whole being in a different emotion.

Gentle, courteous waves lapped shoreward. Kind breezes from the offing rippled the waters to the bank, where they etched graceful undulations and arabesques in sand. Barefoot children fled from the incoming wavelets and chased them gleefully as they withdrew seaward, leaving nothing on the shore but stripes of foam. Like the children, my heart followed the waves till, hypnotized by their monotony, I felt as if I could have walked on their soft surfaces.

Nature harbors within itself the power to evoke sympathetic responses in all of us, and we must be ready to follow as it leads. The motorboat passenger who fights against the rise and fall of the waves becomes seasick; he who joins them unresistingly does not. The way to truly profound intercourse with nature is to understand both the kindly lullaby of the calm sea and the screaming rage of the storm and to accept both.

The howling wind turns up the undersides of the leaves and, bending the clattering branches, makes horrid sounds as it shrieks up the mountainside while another gust hurries to continue the frightening ritual. Fallen leaves fly up, and five or six ruffled birds first strive to huddle together for protection and then, in confusion, follow the leaves.

It is a frightful thing that I cannot see the wind. I can feel it on my skin, and from the frenzy of the leaves on the trees I can guess its direction; but I cannot see it. Nevertheless, it works on my soul in strange ways. Sometimes it evokes memories of deep sadness; sometimes it aggravates anger; and sometimes it heaps on despair till I wonder why and how long I must struggle on. But just as I feel I will sink under the load, the wind inspires me with clarion calls to bravery and steels me to stand boldly like a blighted, but undaunted, tree.

When the wind is gone and remains no more than a dream, becoming meditative and lyrical, I realize that the gem-colored paradise of nature and all of her other guises welcome humanity, even though man be as weak as an ant or as frail as a drenched and wounded butterfly.

I have read many travel comments and discussions of Japanese scenery in which important characteristics were skillfully revealed or in which acute comparisons were made between the Japanese and the Western approaches to nature. I disparage none of these, but in these short introductions to the four sections of photographs my aim 153 has been different. I have wanted to give the reader material for thought and to leave the responsibility for—and the pleasure of—making judgments entirely to him.

I dare say that were I asked to show tourists the scenic wonders of Japan, even if I had an unlimited amount of time, I would be unenthusiastic. My reason is this: Forced to deal with the polite but only casually interested tourist who ceremonially aims his camera at the right things and asks why many places in Japan have strange-sounding names, I would have nothing to say.

On the other hand, should I know that a person had come to this country with nothing but the pleasure of seeing beautiful places in his heart, I would feel differently, because I could rest safe in the knowledge that no explanations from me would be required, or perhaps even wanted. By merely pointing my finger left or right to some lovely grove or hill, I would know that I had fulfilled my obligation. Sadly enough, the things a person treasures in the most subjective chambers of his soul cannot be expressed with facility in words. The guide's sole duty is to point out. Fortunately there are people in all countries who understand this, and to them I could happily show my favorite country lanes, fishing villages, or forests filled with singing birds, which, unaided by me, clearly tell the story of nature in Japan and the way it nurtures the human soul.

And is this not precisely what Mr. Midorikawa is doing for us in this book's photographs? He is telling us to look at the beauties of nature in Japan, at his favorite scenes, and then to look within ourselves for their eternal meaning. Could we find a better guide?

PHOTOGRAPHS

96. Sun over Snow, Shiretoko

97–98. Naruto Current, Seto Inland Sea

99. Sunset, Seto Inland Sea

100. Walls of Aso Crater, Aso

101–2. Mount Tokachi, Daisetsuzan

103. New Mount Showa, Shikotsu-Toya

104. Sakurajima's Main Crater,
                    Kirishima-Yaku

105. The Female Akan Volcano, Akan

106–7. Akan Fuji, Akan

108. Night Sky over Mount Hodaka,
                    Chubu Mountains

109. Mount Aso Crater, Aso

110. Extinct Crater, Aso

111. Mount Neko by Night, Aso

112. Kannon Gorge, Southern Alps

113. Rapids at Oirase in Autumn,
                    Towada-Hachimantai

114. Kegon Falls, Nikko

115. Late Autumn at Lake Chuzenji, Nikko

116. Sunset at Lake Chuzenji, Nikko

117. Ryuzu Falls, Nikko

118. Early Morning, Chubu Mountains

119. Moon over Shore, Kirishima-Yaku

155

On a temple bell,
a butterfly,
sleeping.
　　　　　　—Buson

A camellia fell . . .
a cock crowed . . .
another camellia fell.
　　　　　　—Baishitsu

Falling head over heels
down a bank,
I found violets.
　　　　　　—Bakan

All were silent—
host, and guest,
and white chrysanthemum.
　　　　　　—Ryota

Summer ice—
what are diamonds
compared with this?
—Kiichi

101

The Kiso River rages, the Kiso Mountains smile.
—Meisetsu

106

107

A starlit night—how high the stars! how wide the sky!
　　　　　　　　　　　　　　　　　—Shohaku

In the evening's cool,
someone told us the names of stars.
                                    —Shiki

A summer night, and the moon
leaping from cloud to cloud.
                                    —Ranko

*A willow needs no brush
to paint pictures
on the wind.*
          —Saryu

*After scattering blossoms,
what's left of the wind
blows on to make eddies
in a cloudless sky.*
          —Ki no Tsurayuki

117

Life flows away; people depart; only the moon remains.
—Oemaru

The National Parks of Japan   Michio Oi

A Brief Guide

THE GREAT VARIETY of scenic beauty in Japan, especially as found in the country's national parks, is doubly impressive when one takes into account the fact that so much beauty is compressed into such a small area. For example, the United States has twenty-five times the area of Japan.

It is difficult to describe in words the peculiar quality of the Japanese landscape. To say it consists mainly of three components—volcanic mountain, seaside, and forest—is to be prosaic, while to define its elusive quality as "delicacy" is to repeat a platitude. Instead, then, I would prefer to emphasize the quality of great diversity within a small space—of high mountains, broad plateaus, deep valleys, wide lakes, picturesque marshes, swift rivers, and heavy forests, all within an area slightly smaller than that of the state of California.

Another noteworthy aspect of the Japanese landscape is the harmony that exists between natural beauty and the works of man. Man too is, or should be, a part of nature, and when the physical structures of his civilization harmonize with rather than disfigure the natural landscape, a new sort of beauty comes into existence. In our industrial age we are fortunate to have before us such inspiring examples of this harmony as the Grand Shrines of Ise, the Toshogu Shrine at Nikko, or the terraced hills of the Seto Inland Sea. Surely these should inspire us to find new ways to bring our industrialized civilization more in harmony with nature.

Polluted air and water have taken their toll on Japan's natural beauty, but like other industrialized nations, Japan is beginning to make efforts to halt and reverse this situation. The foliage on a number of islands in the Inland Sea, for example, had been killed off by poisonous factory fumes, but a way has been found to render the gases harmless and now greenery is returning.

It was out of a great love of nature and a desire to preserve it that a system of national parks was first established in Japan in 1934, only half a century after the establishment of the first national park in the world, Yellowstone National Park in the United States. Since that time Japan's national park system has grown to include twenty-three national parks with a total area of over 7,500 square miles, constituting five percent of Japan's total land area.

Most of Japan's national parks are located near population centers and thus provide easily accessible recreation areas for hiking, mountain climbing, skiing, boating, swimming, and the like. Year by year facilities such as inns, hotels, and roads increase 187 in quality. It is estimated that the total number of yearly visits to Japan's national parks is now almost two billion—a large figure even though it doubtless includes a large percentage of repeated visits by the same persons. The tremendous popularity of national parks in Japan is further indicated by a comparison with the United States, where a total of thirty-five national parks are said to have only a billion and a half visitors each year—from a population almost twice as large as Japan's.

In its organization, Japan's national park system as established and administered under the National Park Law differs rather radically from the system of other nations. In the United States and Canada, for example, all the land and facilities in national parks are actually owned by the national government. The Japanese parks, on the other hand, include both public and privately owned land and facilities. Private owners are prevented by law from taking actions that would substantially alter the natural beauty of the area, and the tourist facilities and general preservation of the entire park are closely supervised by the government.

Granted that this system is, from the administrative point of view, inferior to that of outright governmental ownership. Still, in countries like Japan and England with dense populations and limited land area, it is necessary to put the same land to many different uses.

Besides the twenty-three national parks described briefly in the following pages, there are certain other areas that have here been called regional parks. Actually, the national park system of Japan is divided into three categories, roughly paralleling the national, state, and county parks of the United States: 1) The national park (koku-ritsu koen), designated and supervised by the national government. 2) The quasi-national park (kokutei koen), designated by the national government and supervised by the local prefectural government. And 3) the prefectural national park (todofuken-ritsu shizen koen), designated and supervised by the local prefectural government.

Although it is only the first category, the true national parks, that we are treating here, the regional parks also play an important role in the national recreational life. And it should be borne in mind that even the national and regional parks taken together are far from having a monopoly on Japan's natural beauty. In any part of the country the traveler comes across spots of spectacular loveliness: these are the natural heritage of Japan. Surely they should all be preserved, and the national park system is but a small beginning toward this ideal.

A representative sampling of Japan's wealth of natural beauty will be found in the national parks as shown in the photographs in this book. Anyone desiring to visit the parks for himself will find the many tourist bureaus of Japan most helpful in supplying full travel information and making reservations. The following descriptions of the parks, though giving only a summary idea of their principal characteristics, may be of help to the visitor in deciding which of them he would like to see with his own eyes.

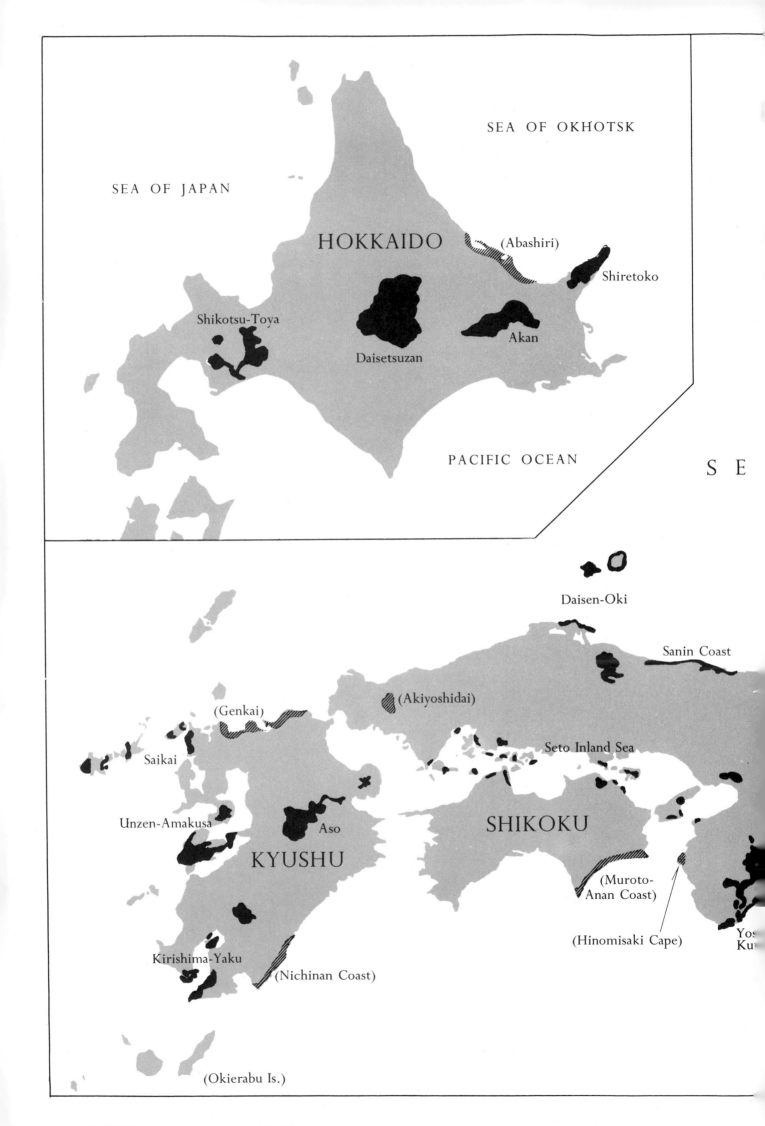

SEA OF OKHOTSK

SEA OF JAPAN

HOKKAIDO

(Abashiri)

Shiretoko

Shikotsu-Toya

Daisetsuzan

Akan

PACIFIC OCEAN

S E

Daisen-Oki

Sanin Coast

(Akiyoshidai)

(Genkai)

Saikai

Seto Inland Sea

Unzen-Amakusa

Aso

SHIKOKU

KYUSHU

(Muroto-
Anan Coast)

Kirishima-Yaku

(Hinomisaki Cape)

Yos
Ku

(Nichinan Coast)

(Okierabu Is.)

THE NATIONAL PARKS OF JAPAN

NOTE: This map shows the 23 national parks of Japan, as of April, 1969, where most of the photographs in this book were taken. Also shown, in parentheses, are a few regional parks and other scenic areas pictured in the book but not included in the following guide.

HOKKAIDO

F JAPAN

Towada-Hachimantai

Rikuchu Coast

Bandai-Asahi

Joshinetsu Heights

Chubu
Mountains

Hakusan

Nikko

H O N S H U

Southern Alps

Chichibu-Tama

e-Shima

Fuji-Hakone-Izu

PACIFIC OCEAN

AKAN

Location: eastern Hokkaido
Prefecture: Hokkaido
Date of designation: December 4, 1934
Area: 87,498 hectares (about 338 sq. mi.)
Photos: 37–38, 105–7

Akan creates the most truly Hokkaido-like mood of all the parks of this northernmost of Japan's main islands. It is a subtle blend of vast landscapes, dense primeval forests, and mystical lakes and bogs steeped in ancient Ainu legend. Its primitive site consists of a larger depression from which rise the volcanoes Kussharo, Mashu, and Akan. The entire park is covered with sub-arctic forests of silver and white fir, and at every turn the eye discerns some new scenic wonder; beginning with the peak that gives the park its name, there is first the black and heavily forested Mount Akan (4,930 ft.) sending columns of smoke into the air, the graceful outlines of Akan Fuji, mysterious Lake Mashu, the expansive shorelines of Lake Kussharo, the secluded mountain recesses in which lie lakes Panketo and Penketo, and Lake Akan famous for its *marimo* (*Tegagropila sauteri*), balls of threadlike algae peculiar to the region.

Perhaps the most convenient aspect of this park is the fact that it can be enjoyed almost entirely from an automobile. Entering from Mount Bihoro (1,647 ft.), the visitor catches a panoramic view of the entire park. From this point one drives by the lovely expanse of Lake Kussharo, and thence through the birch, creeping pine, and azalea forests of the sulphur-mountain range near Kawayu Hot Springs. Rising to the level of Lake Mashu, with Mount Mashu in the background, and going toward Teshikaga, one passes through deep forests on the way to Lake Akan and finally arrives at an elevated observation point from which is seen a splendid view of two lakes and two towering peaks. Several hot-spring resorts—Wakoto, Kawayu, Teshikaga, and Lake Akan—are located along this route, at which visitors may rest and prepare for the remainder of their journey.

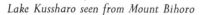

Lake Kussharo seen from Mount Bihoro

ASO

Location: central Kyushu
Prefectures: Kumamoto, Oita
Date of designation: December 4, 1934
Area: 73,060 hectares (about 282 sq. mi.)
Photos: 32, 100, 109–11

This park is best known for Mount Aso itself, the world's largest volcanic crater, from the floor of which tower five volcanic peaks; but also included in the designated area are the slopes and environs of Aso, together with the Kokonoe Range and the range between mounts Yufu and Tsurumi. The Aso crater measures almost 10 miles from east to west and 20 miles from north to south and has a circumference of about 80 miles. Of the five inner peaks—Takadake (the highest, 5,222 feet), Nekodake, Kijima, Eboshi, and Nakadake—only the latter is still active, constantly belching smoke. The best spots from which to view this vast volcanic region are the observation points at Uchinomaki and at Shiroyama in Ichinomiya, where panoramas of great drama extend in all directions and present a grand spectacle of nature.

The Kokonoe Range, of volcanic origin, includes mounts Kuju (the highest, 5,861 ft.), Hossho, Mimata, and Daisen. The grandeur and beauty of the entire region is enhanced by masses of the lovely purple-red *miyama-kirishima* (*Rhododendron kiusianum*).

Mountain climbers and hikers use the following hot-spring resorts and other facilities at the bases of the mountains: Akagawa, Makinoto, Kannojigoku, Chojabaru, Sujiyu, and Hokein. A good highway runs from Beppu to Aso across the highland plains at the bases of mounts Yufu and Tsurumi, makes a circuit of the crater, and descends into Aso Valley.

The Nakadake crater seen from Takadake

193

BANDAI-ASAHI

Location: northern Honshu
Prefectures: Yamagata, Fukushima, Niigata
Date of designation: September 5, 1950
Area: 189,661 hectares (about 732 sq. mi.)
Photos: 8, 11

Bandai-Asahi is divided into three major areas: 1) between Mount Gassan and the Asahi Range, 2) centering on Mount Iide, and 3) between mounts Azuma and Bandai. The wide summit of conical, gently sloping Mount Gassan (6,494 ft.) is covered with Japanese primroses (*Primula nipponica*) and wild poppies. Heavy snows, particularly on the east side of the Paleozoic Asahi mountains, have eroded the slopes and engraved deep marks on the topography. Bears, *kamoshika* (*capriocornis crispus*, a kind of antelope), and monkeys range the wide plain of the Miomote River, which rises on the west side of these mountains.

Mount Iide (6,904 ft.) is largely granite and, like the Asahi Range, is covered with beech forests that provide wild animals with a sheltered habitat.

Mount Bandai (5,966 ft.) erupted in 1887 and the resulting lava flow greatly altered its shape. The Ura-Bandai resort area, created after that eruption, is now very popular in summer because of a number of its features: handsome groves of Japanese cypress, lakes Hibara and Onogawa, and the Akimoto and Goshiki marshes. Lake Inawashiro, in the Omote-Bandai area, is the third largest lake in Japan and is widely used for boating and camping.

The mountain range extending from mounts Nishi Azuma (6,573 ft.) and Higashi Azuma (6,478 ft.) to Mount Adatara (5,576 ft.) is of volcanic origin and includes the active volcano Issaikyo. This area is connected with the Bandai area by roads that are currently being improved to make automobile travel more comfortable and convenient.

Mount Bandai seen across Lake Hibara

CHICHIBU-TAMA

Location: central Honshu, northwest of Tokyo
Prefectures: Saitama, Yamanashi, Nagano, Tokyo
Date of designation: July 10, 1950
Area: 121,600 hectares (about 469 sq. mi.)
Photo: 80

Located near Tokyo, this park gives weary urbanites the rare chance to stroll undisturbed in shaded forests where birds sing. Several peaks of the Kanto Range, composed largely of aqueous and plutonic rocks, comprise an important part of the attractions of the Chichibu and Tama regions: Kimpu (8,512 ft.), Kokushi, Kobushi, Kumotori, and Ryogami, all the latter being about 6,560 feet high.

Heavy rainfall and rich soil make for luxuriant growth of *shirabe* (white Japanese cypress, *Abies veitchii*) and *kome-tsuga* (dwarf hemlock-spruce, *Tsuga diversifolia*) even above the mid-levels of the mountains. Numerous rivers, including the Arakawa, Tamagawa, Fuefuki, and Chikuma, have carved spectacular valleys and gorges throughout the park. Higashi Valley and Shosen Gorge, near the city of Kofu, are famous scenic spots.

Its nearness to the Tokyo-Yokohama metropolitan complex makes this a favorite retreat for hikers, mountain climbers, and picnickers.

The Kanto Range seen from Mount Daibosatsu

CHUBU MOUNTAINS

Location: northern part of central Honshu
Prefectures: Niigata, Toyama, Gifu, Nagano
Date of designation: December 4, 1934
Area: 169,768 hectares (about 655 sq. mi.)
Photos: 24, 26, 108, 118

A mecca for the alpinist, the Chubu Mountains offer white clouds capping towering peaks, snowy valleys receding one after the other in the distance, and in spring, a riot of many kinds of wild flowers.

Occupying part of the central area of Honshu, this park is crossed by several mountain ranges. The Tateyama Range includes Tsurugi (9,850 ft.), Tateyama (9,889 ft.), Yakushi, and Mitsumata-range; the Ushiro Tateyama Range includes Shirouma (9,620 ft.), Karamatsu, Kashima Yarigatake, and Harinoki; the Jonen Range includes Tsubakuro, Jonen, and Otaki; and the Yarihodaka Range runs from Yarigatake (10,430 ft.) to Hodaka (10,463 ft.). In addition to these, the park also has a number of independent volcanic peaks, such as Yake and Norikura (9,925 ft.). Geologically, these mountains are composed largely of Paleozoic strata and plutonic rocks plus Cenozoic igneous rocks and more recent lava.

The Kurobe, Takase, and Azusa rivers have carved deep gorges through these young, rough mountains, and thrilling canyons greet the eye in many places. Especially lovely, in the Kamikochi area, are the fields of larches and willows along the Azusa River (elevation 4,920 ft.), surrounded by mounts Hodaka, Yake, Myojin, and Kasumizawa.

In the vicinity of the Tateyama Range, the visitor can see ice-scoured regions, unusual in Japan; and in the Midagahara, Goshikigahara, and Kumonodaira regions, an abundance of mountain vegetation. Among the extensive wildlife of the park the kamoshika (a kind of antelope) and snow grouse are especially noteworthy.

Mountain-climbing opportunities in these so-called Northern Alps are richly varied, with courses graded into categories for beginning, intermediate, and advanced degrees of difficulty. Although the Kamikochi highlands near Matsumoto and the area around Murodo in Tateyama used to be favorite alpinist haunts, in recent years these areas have been largely taken over by the general tourist.

The triform Mount Hodaka seen from the Azusa River

DAISEN-OKI

Location: the Japan Sea coast, western Honshu
Prefectures: Tottori, Okayama, Shimane
Date of designation: February 1, 1936
Area: 31,927 hectares (about 123 sq. mi.)
Photos: 23, 93–94

This park derives its name from Daisen, the highest peak of the Sanin Mountains, from which one can enjoy a spectacular view of the Shimane Peninsula and the Oki Islands in the Sea of Japan. Daisen (5,678 ft.) is a conical volcano which in some places has the sloping, graceful lines of Mount Fuji and in others is cut by towering cliffs of the alpine kind. Throughout the year, sightseers, mountain climbers, and campers are to be found at Daisenji, Masumizubara, and Kagamiganaru, at the mountain's base, enjoying the many beautiful areas the park offers.

Hirusen, a composite of large, medium, and small volcanoes with spacious plains at their bases, is a favorite of many lovers of nature.

The Oki Islands, divided into the Tozen group and Togo Island, are noted for their dramatically weathered shorelines and cliffs. Especially famous are the Maten Cliffs on Nishi Island, the Red Cliffs of Chiburi Island, and Shirojima and the Jusen Cliffs of Togo Island. In the twelfth century, one Japanese emperor was exiled to the Oki Islands, and each year many visitors come both to see the spectacular scenery and to examine the historical relics.

Other famous places include the splendid architecture of the Grand Shrine of Izumo, one of Shinto's oldest and most sacred spots; the Miho Shrine and the nearby wedded pines; the sea cave of Kugedo at Kaga; and the picturesque promontory of Hinomisaki.

Mount Sanbe, a small volcano of sugar-loaf shape, is a charming sight; and Shigaku Hot Springs and Ukinuno Pond are popular resorts for mountain climbers, campers, and skiers.

Himenoga Pond on Mount Sanbe

197

DAISETSUZAN

Location: central Hokkaido
Prefecture: Hokkaido
Date of designation: December 4, 1934
Area: 231,929 hectares (about 895 sq. mi.)
Photos: 5, 39–40, 101–2

This is the largest of Japan's national parks. Rich in untouched forests, it contains deep, thrilling valleys and canyons and towering mountains such as the Daisetsuzan group (called the roof of Hokkaido), Tomuraushi Volcano, the Tokachi volcanic group to the south of that, and, in the east, soaring Mount Ishikari, composed largely of Paleozoic rock. Mount Daisetsu itself is the main peak of a volcanic group resting on a Paleozoic base composed of andesite and rhyolite. The group measures about 26 miles from north to south and 19 miles east to west and reaches a height of almost 6,600 feet. At its pinnacles is a great plain formed by a volcanic crater. To the south of it towers Mount Asahi (7,511 ft.), the highest mountain on Hokkaido.

The funicular from Soun Gorge and Yukomanbetsu is the most generally used approach to this wild summit, but walking is probably the most exciting and spectacular way to get there, giving one time to enjoy the scenery.

The mountains south of Daisetsuzan—Tomuraushi, Oputateshike, Biei, and the active volcano Tokachi—are a rich treasure house of wild mountain flowers. From Mount Mikuni in the east corner of the park, one can enjoy a view of mounts Yuni-Ishikari, Otofuke, and Ishikari, parts of the Paleozoic andesite and granite formations from which spring two large rivers, the Ishikari and the Tokachi. The entire area is covered in dense forest.

Craggy columns of rhyolite bastion the sides of Ishikari Canyon, into which plummet Obako, Kobako, Ginga, and Ryusei falls. The Hagoromo Falls plunges into the Tennin Gorge of the Chubetsu River, and in the south of the park is the extremely deep lake Shikaribetsu, noted both for its handsome shoreline and for its hot springs. Other hot-spring resorts are found at Soun Gorge, Aizan Valley, Yukomanbetsu, Tennin Gorge, Biei, Fukiage, Nukabira, and Yamada.

The Daisetsuzan group seen from the skiing grounds at Mount Tokachi

FUJI-HAKONE-IZU

Location: central Honshu, west of Tokyo
Prefectures: Kanagawa, Yamanashi, Shizuoka, Tokyo
Date of designation: February 1, 1936
Area: 122,309 hectares (about 472 sq. mi.)
Photos: 20, 22

This extensive park boasts the grandeur of world-famous Mount Fuji, the Hakone volcanic belt, the Fuji volcanic belt, the Izu Peninsula (with its splendid beaches and rocky coastline), and the volcanic Seven Izu Islands stretching some 150 miles out into the Pacific.

Japan's highest mountain at 12,385 feet and one of the most elegantly shaped anywhere, Mount Fuji slopes gracefully and symmetrically on all sides. Around it are five beautiful lakes, including Lake Kawaguchi, and its sides are covered with a rich variety of forests, including the firs of Oshino and the needle-bearing evergreens of Aokigahara. The Fuji group includes more than sixty subsidiary volcanoes, such as mounts Hoei and Omuro, and has a surface pitted with glacial holes and lava formations. Thrilling views of Fuji are obtained from the nearby Misaka group, Mitsu Pass, Koyodai, and Tenshigadake.

The Hakone Mountains are a classic example of a double-volcano group, with a ring of outer peaks—Myojin, Kintoki, etc.—and an inner ring near the central crater—Kami, Komagatake, etc. Between these rings lie the lake Ashinoko, formed from a volcanic crater, and the volcanic highland plain of Sengokubara. Being near Tokyo and Yokohama, this area began developing as an outdoor recreation area several decades ago, and it offers a wide range of hotels, good roads, funicular railways, and ropeways.

The range of volcanic mountains running down the middle of the Izu Peninsula is traversed by a good highway and provides many startling and inclusive views of Mount Fuji. But the peninsula is also scenically interesting in its own right, particularly the rugged western coastline, and attracts many visitors throughout the year.

All of the Izu Islands are volcanoes that have thrust their tops out of the sea. Even today, Mount Mihara on Oshima and Oyama on Miyake-jima continue to erupt from time to time. Mikura Island is famous for its majestic cliffs and forests of box, whereas Hachijo Island (the southernmost) is noted for its subtropical vegetation. The exposed quartz boulders of Nii, Shikine, and Kozu islands fascinate with seemingly endless variety. All the Izu Islands are popular resort areas.

Mount Fuji seen from Oshino

HAKUSAN

Location: northern part of central Honshu
Prefectures: Toyama, Ishikawa, Fukui, Gifu
Date of designation: November 12, 1962
Area: 47,402 hectares (about 831 sq. mi.)
Photos: 48, 78

The top of Hakusan ("white mountain"), long a favorite scenic attraction of northern Honshu, is covered with creeping pine and a wide variety of colorful flowers, creating a mountainous atmosphere of such beauty and purity as to justify the mountain's name. The several ranges passing through the park include mounts Ogasa, Myoho, Hakusan, Bessan, Sannomine, and Dainichi.

Hakusan is, in fact, a composite mountain, the main peak of which, Gozenmine (8,863 ft.), consists of lava pierced with layers of Mesozoic material and eight craters at its top. One of these is now Lake Senja, the only subarctic lake in Japan; even in summer, most of the lake is ice locked. High-altitude flora carpets the upper levels, and forests of white fir, beech, and Japanese oak cover the lower slopes of the mountain.

At Iwama Hot Springs, at the foot of the mountain, there are many geysers, and in the vicinity of Yunotani are virtual forests of Jurassic fossils. One of the most important attractions of the Oshira River is the Shiramizu waterfall.

Many people find this park an attractive camping and mountain-climbing site the year round, and it is also popular in winter for its good skiing facilities. Popular lodging areas include Ichinose and Iwama Hot Springs, both in Ishikawa Prefecture; Oshirakawa, in Gifu Prefecture; and Heisenji, in Fukui Prefecture.

The Central Alps viewed across Mount Onanji's Green Pond and a sea of clouds

200

ISE-SHIMA

Location: central Honshu, south of Nagoya
Prefecture: Mie
Date of designation: November 20, 1946
Area: 52,036 hectares (about 201 sq. mi.)
Photo: 50

Although the park includes a stretch of the gentle coastline of the eastern side of the Kii Peninsula, its most important features are the Grand Shrines of Ise and the stately forest surrounding them. Composed of the Inner and Outer Precincts, the Ise Shrines, long closely associated with the imperial family, are a magnificent blend of simple architecture and magnificent forests, some of which are carefully tended and others left untouched.

The complex coast is composed of four bays—Toba, Matoya, Ago, and Gokasho—all of which are themselves richly varied in topography. Off the shore are numerous small islands. Countless rafts for the production of cultured pearls characterize the sheltered bays.

Hotels and inns at Toba and Kashikojima cater to the many tourists, both Japanese and foreign, who visit this famous park all year round.

Hamayu *flowers* (Crinum asiaticum) *on Oshima island*

JOSHINETSU HEIGHTS

Location: northern part of central Honshu
Prefectures: Gumma, Niigata, Nagano
Date of designation: September 7, 1949
Area: 188,915 hectares (about 729 sq. mi.)
Photos: 25, 46, 76–77, 79

Winter sports, particularly skiing, are very popular in the highlands at Shiga, Sugadaira, Asama, and Myoko, all of which are volcanic regions.

The park is divided into two main sections: that containing Mount Asama, the Sugadaira and Shiga heights, the Tanigawa Mountains, and Mount Naeba; and that featuring mounts Myoko and Kurohime and the Togakushi Mountains.

Mount Asama (8,338 ft.), the largest active volcano in Japan, still smokes and erupts from time to time. On its southeastern slopes is the famous summer resort Karuizawa; and on its northern slope, the devastated lava flow called Onioshidashi. Sugadaira Heights, on the side of Mount Azumaya, is a popular ski resort, and many other ski slopes dot the entire region from Shiga Heights to Mount Shirane and the towns of Kusatsu and Manza, making this the most extensive skiing area in the country. The sides of Mount Naeba (7,036 ft.), a conical, gently sloping volcano, are covered with sedge and dotted with hot springs.

Unlike the foregoing mountains, the Tanigawa Range is composed largely of aqueous and plutonic rock in sheer alpine cliffs. Since it is nearer the Tokyo-Yokohama region, many mountain climbers use this section of the park.

Mounts Myoko (8,023 ft.), Kurohime, and Iizuna are gently sloping conical volcanoes, with excellent ski runs on the lower slopes. The Togakushi Shrine on the craggy, boulder-strewn side of Mount Togakushi adds a note of human culture to the natural scene.

Numerous hot-spring resorts in the areas of Mount Asama, Shiga Heights, and mounts Myoko and Togakushi greatly increase the recreational value of the park.

A view of Ikenodaira in the Myoko region

KIRISHIMA-YAKU

Location: southernmost Kyushu
Prefectures: Miyazaki, Kagoshima
Date of designation: March 16, 1934
Area: 55,231 hectares (about 213 sq. mi.)
Photos: 63–64, 104, 119

Located the farthest south of all the parks, Kirishima-Yaku boasts flora unlike that found elsewhere. The Kirishima Mountains include several volcanoes of the standard conical form. Kinko Bay is noted for its spectacular beauty, and Yaku Island offers unusual and diverse vegetation.

Resembling the crater-pocked face of the moon, the Kirishima group contains twenty-three volcanoes in all, including Karakuni (the highest at 5,576 ft.), Takachiho (according to mythology, the first Japanese emperor descended from heaven at this spot), and Shinmoe, as well as Lake Onami. Near the tops of the mountains grow the great expanses of wild mountain azalea for which the area is famous, and the bases are covered with great forests of shii (Lithocarpus edulis, related to the oak), oak, and red pine.

Although there are convenient roads in the area, the best way to see the craters is on foot from any of these hot-spring resorts: Ebino, in Miyazaki Prefecture; and Hayashida and Enno, in Kagoshima Prefecture.

The volcano on Sakura Island in Kinko Bay has erupted on numerous occasions, and each lava flow and its incursions into the vegetation cover are clearly distinguishable. On the tip of the Satsuma Peninsula are the Ibusuki Hot Springs, noted for the quantity of their steam output, and nearby are such points of interest as Cape Nagasakibana, Lake Ikeda, and the conical volcano Kaimon. Forests of Chinese fan palm (Livistonia chinensis) cover the tip of Cape Sata at the end of the Osumi Peninsula.

The island of Yakushima, 37 miles south of Cape Sata, is mountainous—its highest peak, Miyanoura, rises to 6,347 feet—and covered with forests of huge cedars, firs, and hemlock spruce, some of which are over a thousand years old. Like Shiretoko at the far northern end of Japan, Yakushima is wild and primeval, and through its forests roam herds of deer and packs of wild monkeys.

Cape Sata lighthouse at the tip of the Osumi Peninsula

NIKKO

Location: eastern Honshu, northeast of Tokyo
Prefectures: Fukushima, Tochigi, Gumma, Niigata
Date of designation: December 4, 1934
Area: 140,698 hectares (about 543 sq. mi.)
Photos: 1–3, 17–19, 21, 45, 47, 114–17

Perhaps to a greater extent than any other national park, Nikko manifests the true characteristics of Japanese scenery: complex topography, highly varied flora, and rich yet subtle beauty. Located in the Nasu volcanic region to the north of the Kanto Plains, Nikko Park consists of three major sections—the district centering on Oze, the Nikko Mountains, and the area between mounts Takahara and Nasu.

Oze Plain, between mounts Hiuchi (7,695 ft.) and Shibutsu (7,311 ft.), is the largest high-altitude hot-spring region in Japan, with an average altitude of 4,600 feet; it measures 1.2 miles from north to south and 3 miles east to west. Its numerous ponds and lakes are thick with *mizu-basho* ("aquatic plantains," *Lysichiton camtschatense*) and *Nikko-kisuge* ("Nikko floating sedge," *Hemerocallis middendorffii*); and the numerous hot springs in the Oze Marsh are famous for their unusual butterflies and dragonflies.

The Nikko Mountains include Okushirane (8,453 ft.), a volcanic group made up of mounts Nantai, Taro, and Nyoho, as well as highland meadows, marshes, waterfalls, valleys, and, of course, the noted architectural splendors of the Toshogu, the mausoleum of Ieyasu, the founder of the Tokugawa shogunate. Among its plains are Senjogahara and Kirifuri Heights. Lakes Chuzenji and Yunoko are famous; and among the numerous waterfalls the most popular is Kegon, fed by Lake Chuzenji, although also well known are Yutaki, Ryuzu, and Kirifuri. Visitors from abroad are usually most impressed by the harmony existing between the elaborately carved and gilded dazzle of the Toshogu Shrine and the forest of towering cryptomerias surrounding it.

The volcanic region between mounts Takahara and Nasu is a favorite outdoor recreation site because of its highlands, hot springs, ski facilities, and golf courses.

Aquatic plants in Oze Marsh

204

RIKUCHU COAST

Location: northern Honshu, facing the Pacific
Prefectures: Iwate, Miyagi
Date of designation: May 2, 1955
Area: 11,584 hectares (about 45 sq. mi.)
Photos: 15, 72-73

Being an island country, Japan has many beautiful stretches of seacoast, but probably none is so moving in the splendor of sea-worn cliffs and the wheeling of gulls and petrels as the Rikuchu Coast, whose islands are often called the Alps of the sea. The park consists of a belt of coastline some 93 miles long stretching from Cape Kitayama, in Iwate Prefecture, to Kesennuma Bay, in Miyagi Prefecture.

North of the town of Miyako, the shoreline is marked with high promontories: the rhododendron-topped cliffs of Cape Kitayama, the Great Sanno Rock, the observation platform at Cape Taroma, and the Reefs of Sakabe, where gulls breed. One of the most popular attractions of the coastline is Jodo Beach, which, composed entirely of quartz rather than of lava sand, is white instead of the gray that typifies most Japanese beaches.

South of Miyako, the coast is sedimentary and elaborately indented with bays and inlets. Their capes, which face the Pacific, tower above the sea in cliffs ranging as high as 984 feet at the sea-worn Akahira Cliff, near the base of Mount Karo.

The island of Oshima in Funagoshi Bay, covered with red pine, camphor, and *hisakaki* (*Eurya japonica,* of the camellia family), has a huge granite terrace called the "Thousand-Mat Shelf," referring to Japanese *tatami* flooring. All the capes, bays, and promontories of this area have distinguishing characteristics. For instance, Sankan Island at the mouth of Kamaishi Bay is famous as a breeding ground for the long-tailed shearwater.

Obviously, the best way to tour this park is by boat from one of the bays—Taro, Miyako, Kamaishi, or Kesennuma—but hiking is also satisfactory when the waves are too high for boats.

Rock formations in the Pacific off Jodo Beach

SAIKAI

Location: northwestern Kyushu
Prefecture: Nagasaki
Date of designation: March 16, 1955
Area: 24,324 hectares (about 94 sq. mi.)
Photos: 34, 57–58, 67

More than four hundred islands in the East China Sea—including the Goto Archipelago, the Hirado Islands, and the Kujuku Islands off Kitamatsuura Peninsula—are the main components of this spacious park whose name means "western sea." It lies at the westernmost tip of Japan.

The Goto group includes five main islands—Fukue, Kuga, Naru, Wakamatsu, and Nakadori—and numerous smaller islands, all formed, on an aqueous-rock base, by complicated convolutions of the earth. Outstanding among many lovely views in the area are the following: the layers of Paleozoic rock exposed in the weathered cliff of Tamanoura on Fukue Island, the half-eroded and sea-carved volcano on Saga Island, and the Wakamatsu Straits created from sedimentary rock between the islands of Wakamatsu and Nakadori.

Although geologically similar to the Goto group, the islands of Hirado are distinguished by the old fishing town of Hirado and, west of it, the columnar grain of the granite cliffs on Ajika Island.

The sedimentary shore on the west side of the Kitamatsuura Peninsula undulates violently, and there are many small islands nearby. The Southern Kujuku Islands, near Sasebo, are especially attractive because of their undisturbed natural setting.

Although beautiful sights abound throughout the area, at present visitors tend to congregate only at Hirado and the Southern Kujuku group, but the Goto chain is also worthy of attention.

The Goto Archipelago seen from a plane

206

SANIN COAST

Location: western Honshu, on the Sea of Japan
Prefectures: Kyoto, Hyogo, Tottori
Date of designation: July 15, 1963
Area: 8,996 hectares (about 35 sq. mi.)
Photos: 27, 81–82

One of the loveliest seashore parks in Japan, Sanin stretches from Amino, on the Sea of Japan coast of Kyoto Metropolitan Prefecture, to the sand dunes of Tottori, 47 miles away. The subtle beauty of the undulating shoreline is enhanced by a wide variety of stone formations in lava, plutonic rocks, and Tertiary-period materials. Among the numerous caves and natural tunnels that distinguish this shoreline, the tunnels of Tsurigane and Juji are best known.

Although many points of interest are in the park—including Kumihama Bay and Gembu Cavern, Takeno Shore, Kasumi Shore, Tajima Mihonoura, Uradome Shore—the most important single attraction is Tottori Dunes, the nation's longest, covering an area measuring over half a mile wide by ten miles long.

Anglers and bathers frequenting the park usually lodge at Kinosaki, Hamasaka, Yumura, Tottori City, or some of the other hot springs in the neighborhood.

Sand dunes at Hamasaka

207

SETO INLAND SEA

Location: between Honshu, Shikoku, and Kyushu
Prefectures: Wakayama, Hyogo, Okayama, Hiroshima,
Yamaguchi, Tokushima, Kagawa, Ehime, Fukuoka, Oita
Date of designation: March 16, 1934
Area: 65,930 hectares (about 254 sq. mi.)
Photos: 28–31, 51, 54–56, 83–88, 91–92, 97–99

Water flowing as fast as a river, islands dotting the surface, and on the shores terraced rice fields and small harbor towns that over countless years have established harmony between Man and Nature—such is the characteristic scenery of Japan's Inland Sea, called the Seto Inland Sea in Japanese. Within the area bounded by the Kitan and Naruto straits on the east and those of Kammon and Bunyo on the west, there are some six hundred large and small islands, not counting innumerable islets.

The Inland Sea area is a depression zone with fault lines crossing it like the markings of a checkerboard. In some places deep cave-ins form whirlpools and rapids, whereas in other areas, lesser sinkage has left mountaintops in the form of islands. The geologically complicated topography is mainly plutonic granite, though here and there signs of ancient volcanic activity vary the scenery.

Some of the loveliest of the island groups are the Bisan group (in the mid-reaches of the sea) and the Seven Islands of Kutsuna. The Geiyo group (toward the western end of the sea) is made up of islands so large that the spaces between them resemble major straits.

Here is a breakdown of some of the major scenic attractions by prefectures, starting near Osaka and proceeding around the shores of the sea counterclockwise: WAKAYAMA: Shinwakanoura; Tomogashima. HYOGO: Mount Rokko; Awaji Island; Cape Ako. OKAYAMA: the shoreline from Shibukawa to Mount Washu; Shiraishi Island; Ushimado. HIROSHIMA: Sensui Island; Mount Noro; Miyajima. YAMAGUCHI: Murozumi; Mount Taika; Kammon Straits. OITA: Kunisaki Peninsula; Hime Island; Mount Takasaki. EHIME: Seven Islands of Kutsuna; Omi Island; Kurushima Straits; Sakurai Shore. KAGAWA: Goshikidai; Yashima; Kanka Valley on Shodo Island. TOKUSHIMA: Naruto Straits.

Thus to list but a few of the principal sights of the area unfortunately does not suggest the unsurpassed beauty of the Inland Sea, and even a book of many pages could hardly begin to do justice to its loveliness. Anyone who visits even a small part of the Inland Sea will never forget it.

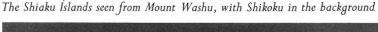

The Shiaku Islands seen from Mount Washu, with Shikoku in the background

SHIKOTSU-TOYA

Location: southwestern Hokkaido
Prefecture: Hokkaido
Date of designation: May 16, 1949
Area: 98,660 hectares (about 381 sq. mi.)
Photo: 103

Though less wild than Shiretoko or Daisetsuzan, this park boasts volcanic scenery of a more recent era and is, fortunately, much more accessible to such population centers as Sapporo, Otaru, Tomakomai, and Muroran. The park's lakes, all formed by natural volcanic depressions, include Shikotsu, Kuttara, and Toya. The source of the Toyohira River is located to the northwest of Lake Shikotsu. Mount Yotei (6,209 ft.) rises about 12 miles north of Lake Toya. In the vicinity of Lake Shikotsu, a natural crater lake, are the volcanoes Tarumae (3,359 ft.), with its crown of rounded hills; Fuppushi; and Eniwa. Not far away is Lake Okotanpe. Lake Kuttara, an almost perfectly round crater lake, is near the famous hot-spring resort Noboribetsu, which has an awesome canyon of steam and hot-mud geysers called Hell Valley.

Islands dot the center of Lake Toya, and the distant view of Mount Yotei, with Nakajima island in the foreground, is cheerful and lovely.

On the south shore is the small volcano Usu (2,378 ft.), which is composed of lava hills called Big Usu, Little Usu, and an auxiliary volcano called Yosomi.

On the east slope of Mount Usu is Showa New Mountain, the region's most recent volcano, which erupted for the first time in 1943 and by 1944 had raised a lava hill 492 feet above the surrounding countryside. It is extremely valuable in the study of volcanic activity.

A range of mountains about 3,200 feet high runs through the area, includes mounts Sapporo, Soranuma, and Izari, and gives rise to the Toyohira River. It is famous for its andesite and rock-cluster walled valleys.

Mount Yotei, similar in shape to the world-famous Fuji, is widely known for the variety of wild mountain plants growing near its summit.

Among the many hot-spring resorts in the area, Noboribetsu, Jozankei, and Toya are most popular. Skiing is good in the Jozankei area.

The west face of Showa New Mountain

SHIRETOKO

Location: eastern Hokkaido
Prefecture: Hokkaido
Date of designation: June 1, 1964
Area: 41,375 hectares (about 160 sq. mi.)
Photos: 7, 35–36, 68–69, 96

Occupying most of the Shiretoko Peninsula and facing the Sea of Okhotsk, Shiretoko Park appeals to lovers of distant journeys and primitive places. The peninsula itself is composed largely of such new Tertiary-layer andesite volcanic peaks as Unabetsu, Onnebetsu, Rausu, and Shiretoko, all of which are part of the Kurile volcanic belt. Myriad clumps of mountain plants grace the high levels of the mountains, and there are many brown bears in the forests of silver fir and white fir. Cormorants and gulls dip and sweep in and around the unbroken line of towering cliffs, cascading falls, and jagged boulders ranked along the seashore.

Primitive scenes of this kind characterize the park, and the most convenient way to enjoy them is to approach the peninsula by boat from nearby Rausu or Utoro. Recently, however, sightseers have begun to hike across Mount Rausu (5,448 ft.).

Ice floes in the Sea of Okhotsk seen from Iwaobetsu

SOUTHERN ALPS

Location: central Honshu, west of Tokyo
Prefectures: Nagano, Yamanashi, Shizuoka
Date of designation: June 1, 1964
Area: 35,799 hectares (about 138 sq. mi.)
Photo: 112

Three mountain systems traverse this second-largest mountain park in Japan: the Kai-Koma system, stretching from Mount Nokogiri to Komagatake (9,725 ft.) and Mount Hoo; the Shirane system, including Japan's second-highest mountain, Kitadake (10,470 ft.), Ainotake, and Notoritake; and finally the Akaishi system, including Senjodake (9,991 ft.), Shiomitake (9,994 ft.), mounts Arakawa and Akaishi (10,234 ft.), and Mount Tekari.

Although the three peaks that make up the Hoo group—Jizo, Kannon, and Yakushi (the names of three Buddhist deities)—are largely granite, mounts Shirane and Akaishi are composed largely of such Paleozoic rocks as hornstone, sandstone, and argillite. The mountainsides and valley walls are covered in stately forests of beech, a kind of spruce (*Picea jezoensis*), fir, and hemlock-spruce.

The area is much favored by mountain climbers, most of whom begin their arduous climbs from such bases as Hirogawara or Nishiyama hot springs, both in Yamanashi Prefecture; Akagawara or Kashio, both in Nagano Prefecture; or Igawa, in Shizuoka Prefecture. There are hotels or inns at all these places.

The Shirane system seen from above the city of Enzan; horizon, left to right: Notoritake, Ainotake, and Kitadake

TOWADA-HACHIMANTAI

Location: northern Honshu
Prefectures: Aomori, Akita, Iwate
Date of designation: February 1, 1936
Area: 83,351 hectares (about 322 sq. mi.)
Photos: 9–10, 12–14, 16, 41–44, 70–71, 74–75, 113

The wildest and richest in volcanic scenery and wild flowers of all the parks on the main island of Honshu, this consists of two regions: from Mount Hakkoda to Lake Towada; and, some 25 miles to the south, the heights of Hachimantai and Mount Iwate.

Mount Hakkoda is actually a volcanic group centering around the Hakkoda peak (5,196 ft.) and composed largely of pyroxene andesite. The sides of the mountain provide excellent ski slopes, where skiers have the added pleasure of enjoying the beauty of white fir and mountain birch bending under heaps of snow and ice. Japanese primrose (*Primula nipponica*) and a kind of wild rose (*Betula ermani*) grow near the summit.

A typical double-crater lake, Towada is surrounded by banks richly decked in beech and Japanese oak. The Oirase River, which flows from the lake, races along in foaming rapids in the very midst of which stand small islands and clumps of trees in a landscape of the subtle kind often found in Japanese painting.

Highways from Aomori and from Hanawa, in Akita Prefecture, facilitate comfortable touring. The best season to visit Towada is autumn, when the colored foliage is at its brightest. Hot-spring resorts along the highways in the area include Sugayu, Tsuta, Sarukura, and Oide (near Lake Towada).

Hachimantai is a gently sloping, flat-topped volcanic structure dotted with steam vents and ponds and covered with a primeval forest of Aomori white fir. Mount Iwate, on the other hand, is a conical volcano (6,694 ft.) with a large central crater, but it too is covered with white fir and mountain birch. Another similarly shaped volcano, Mount Koma (5,369 ft.), located in the southern extremity of the park, has an unusual covering of such high-altitude plants as the *iwa-bukuro* (*Pentstemon frutescens*, related to the beardtongue) and the *koma-kusa* (*Dicentra peregrina*, a kind of wild poppy).

There are many rustic hot-spring resorts and some of them, such as Goshogake, Fuke, and Toshichi, provide hot-mud health treatments.

Lake Towada seen from Mount Towada

UNZEN-AMAKUSA

Location: *western coast of central Kyushu*
Prefectures: *Nagasaki, Kumamoto, Kagoshima*
Date of designation: *March 16, 1934*
Area: *25,665 hectares (about 99 sq. mi.)*
Photos: *60, 62*

This combination mountain-and-seaside park is divided into two parts: Mount Unzen, a compound volcano on Shimabara Peninsula; and to the south, across Hayasaki Straits, the Amakusa Islands. Unzen, which includes such neo-Paleolithic volcanic peaks as Kinugasa, Kusembe, and Fuken, abounds in geysers and hot springs and has a number of fine observation points from which to admire the far-reaching scene. The long-established hot-spring resort of Unzen, on top of and almost in the middle of the volcanic group, offers a number of hotels and inns.

The Amakusa Islands consist of two main islands—Kami and Shimo—and the smaller islands of Matsushima and Goshonoura, all of which contribute to the placid, inland-sea atmosphere of the region. The strikingly eroded cliffs of the Ushibuka coast face the East China Sea.

Many historical relics of the Christian rebellion of the mid-seventeenth century attract great attention. A recently completed bridge from Kyushu to Kamishima, the upper island, makes touring convenient.

Sakitsu port on Amakusa, with its Catholic church in the foreground

213

YOSHINO-KUMANO

Location: central and southern part
of the Kii Peninsula, south of Osaka
Prefectures: Mie, Nara, Wakayama
Date of designation: February 1, 1936
Area: 55,936 hectares (about 216 sq. mi.)
Photos: 52–53

A lack of volcanic mountains characterizes this park, which includes hills, forests, and rivers. Mount Yoshino, in the northern part of the park, is famous for its cherry trees and for historic remains dating from the fourteenth century, when the Japanese court was split into two rival factions, each with its own emperor, one of whom established his court in this region. The mountains extending from Mount Omine to Odaigahara are largely aqueous rock. Odaigahara itself is a semiflat plain with an elevation of 4,920 feet. Handsome forests of cypress and fir cover the hills. The Kitayama River, which has its source within the park, is a continuous drama of whirling waters and rapids.

At Torohatcho, there are deep eddies in the river, above which cliffs rise high and stony to create the kind of scenic composition for which Japan is noted.

The southern portion of the park lies along the southeastern side of the Kii Peninsula facing the Kumano Channel and has a lovely shoreline. At Onigashiro tall weathered and seaworn cliffs of quartz confront the sea. The many offshore islands of Katsuura and the stone pillars at Kushimoto are included in the park, as also are the cape Shionomisaki (the southernmost tip of Honshu) and three famous peaks, Hongu, Shingu, and Nachi. The famous Nachi Falls are located on the latter.

The Omine and Odaigahara regions are popular with mountain climbers, while the seashore and the Torohatcho areas boast fine hiking courses.

Fallen Yoshino cedars at Odaigahara

214

Notes on the Photographs   Yoichi Midorikawa

MANY YEARS AGO, as I flew from Cairo to Athens over the almost fearsome blue of the Mediterranean, where white clouds billowed in the clear sky, I wrote my eldest daughter that I was now observing the sea Botticelli's newborn Venus had sailed in a seashell. At the same time, I was nostalgically reminded of the richly varied natural scenery of the Japanese islands, stretching from subtropic to subarctic regions. It was at that moment that I resolved to devote the rest of my life to making a photographic record of the beauty of my native land. Thus began a quest that has taken me and my camera to coral reefs, snowy plains, and many other inspiringly lovely parts of Japan. This book represents a partial harvest of my efforts, and it is indeed only a part, since these photographs, confined largely to views of national parks, show but a fraction of the beauty of this land.

The following notes are my personal comments on the individual photographs. I hope that something of my deep feeling for "these splendored isles" may be seen both here and in my photographs.

NOTE: In most cases the second element of the main, capitalized caption gives the name of the national park in which the scene is located, and this name may be used to refer back to the alphabetized guide to the national parks of Japan, where more information on the area will be found. In the few cases of regional parks or other scenic areas not included in the guide, a general indication of location is given in parentheses.

1. KEGON FALLS THROUGH BLOSSOMS, NIKKO. A prehistoric eruption of Mount Nantai blocked the flow of the Daiya River and formed Lake Chuzenji, which now empties through one of the most famous falls and gorges in Japan, Kegon. At the bottom of the cliff, water from the falls joins the old course of the Daiya and flows into the Kinugawa river. The Akechi Plateau, an excellent observation point for viewing lake, falls, and gorge, is reached by a ropeway and an additional climb on foot of about 300 yards.

2. WILD RHODODENDRON, NIKKO. My trip to the Akechi Plateau was made in early spring when most buds were still closed and a chill nipped the air; but the lovely pink blossoms of the *yashio* (*Rhododendron albrechti*) were already blooming in a grove, announing the nearness of true springtime. Also visible from this area, in addition to Lake Chuzenji and the Kegon Falls, are mounts Nantai and Tsukuba and the Shirane Range.

3. FALLEN LEAVES ON LAKE CHUZENJI, NIKKO. Scarlet leaves floating on the brilliant azure of Lake Chuzenji in the autumn epitomize the feeling of the season. Although the lake—over 4,000 feet above sea level, 14.3 miles in periphery, and 558 feet at its deepest—is considered especially lovely in both early spring and fall, I find the season of falling leaves most appealing.

4. "CORAL GRASS" AT LAKE NOTORO, ABASHIRI REGIONAL PARK (northeastern coast of Hokkaido). Across a hill northwest of Abashiri lies Lake Notoro, which, with almost 20 miles of shoreline, ranks fifth in size among Hokkaido's many lakes. The lake is slightly over 7 feet at its deepest and opens into the Sea of Okhotsk at Cape Notoro. Along its marshy western shore grows the flaming red grass called *sango-so* ("coral grass"), intensifying the deep blue of the autumn skies above the lake.

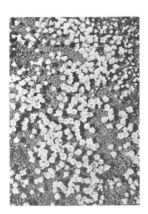

5. BLOSSOMS OF "BOULDER PLUM," DAISETSUZAN. One late June, I was staying in the hot-spring region of Daisetsu Heights, and when I left my inn for a climb, all of the Ezo spruces were still heaped with snow. Even above the great forest, snow lay at the bases of the birch trees, though green buds had begun to appear among their twisted branches. Near the top of the mountain, however, the snow had melted and the *iwa-ume* ("boulder plum," *Diapensia lapponica*) was in bloom, nestled among the rocks.

6. LILIES OF THE VALLEY AT LAKE NOTORO, ABASHIRI REGIONAL PARK (northeastern coast of Hokkaido). The dainty white flowers and broad green leaves of the lily of the valley, the flower symbol of Hokkaido, thrive audaciously in climes too inhospitable for most plants. The blooming season varies from the north to the south of the island, but at Lake Notoro they are at their best in late June.

7. SPRING AT IWAOBETSU, SHIRETOKO. The northernmost outpost of habitability on the island of Hokkaido, until a few years ago even Iwaobetsu was almost totally inaccessible for most of the year. In winter, ice and snow block the passes leading to the area; and in late June, when early summer has already come to most of Japan, here snow still lingers in mountain gorges, and the Ezo dandelion (*Taraxacum officinale*) has just begun to bloom.

8. AUTUMN COLORS AT GOSHIKI MARSH, BANDAI-ASAHI. When Mount Bandai erupted about eighty years ago, countless large and small lakes and marshes were formed in the vicinity, including lakes Hibara and Onogawa and Akimoto Marsh. Though much smaller than these, Goshiki Marsh is noteworthy for the way the composition of its bottom colors the water emerald, blue, and vermilion—hues that in autumn are echoed by the surrounding forests.

9. AUTUMN AT MOUNT MIKURA, TOWADA-HACHIMANTAI. Lake Towada, with some 28 miles of shoreline, is a squarish body of water divided into sections by the two peninsulas that jut into it, Mikura and Nakayama. Mount Mikura drops into the lake in a precipitous cliff of red and brown pumice. On its lower slopes the autumn reds, greens, and golds of the trees are as gorgeous as rich brocade.

10. SAME. Surrounding the deep azure clarity of Lake Towada there is a virtual sea of dazzlingly colored autumn trees, which reach their breathtaking peak of beauty on about the twentieth of October.

11. HIGHLAND AUTUMN, BANDAI-ASAHI. Eighty years ago when Mount Bandai erupted, the large, old trees in the area were submerged in the waters of newly formed Lake Hibara; but a crop of young trees, smaller plants, and pampas grass soon took root in the lava soil of the highlands created by the volcano. Today this restful forest is most beautiful in autumn when the leaves are gilded and breezes ruffle the silver feather tops of the grasses.

12. PRIMEVAL AUTUMN, TOWADA-HACHIMANTAI. I left my inn at Utarube early one morning in the middle of autumn to climb Mount Towada. Since I am a poor climber, I took my time and leisurely enjoyed the fall leaves and towering trees in the early light. Then after two hours of walking, I reached the pinnacle of the mountain, where a sweeping view of Lake Towada and the Hakkoda Mountains awaited me.

13. GOLDEN LEAVES ON TSUTA MARSH, TOWADA-HACHIMANTAI. About ten minutes from Yakeyama on the road to Mount Hakkoda, one comes upon an inn and a single shop set in a lovely grove of beech trees. This little hot-spring retreat, called Tsuta, was a favorite haunt of the famous nineteenth-century writer Keigetsu Omachi. In the marsh, set amidst hot springs and surrounded by mountains, the cycle of nature quietly follows its course. A mood of calm and gentleness pervades the placid waters and rustling trees, most lovely in the autumn.

14. OTAKI FALLS, TOWADA-HACHIMANTAI. The water flowing from Lake Towada flashes silver at some spots along its 9-mile course and at others seems hidden by tunnels of maples. The imposing falls, located at Oirase midway in the river's course from Nenokuchi to Yakeyama, capture the golds and yellows of autumn leaves in their dancing waters. This scene and another section of the stream, where the waters are said to be "like a demon in fury," are among my favorites in the area.

15. WATER REFLECTIONS AT CAPE OKAMA, RIKUCHU COAST. Okamazaki cape, jutting out between Yamada and Funakoshi bays in Iwate Prefecture, is serrate and complicated in outline, as is the entire coastline. On the clear, late-November day when I went to photograph the area, the mystic blue of the deep sea reflected back the russets and creams of the sheer cliffs.

218

16. SPRING SNOW IN DAIKOKU FOREST, TOWADA-HACHIMAN-TAI. In the gently undulating highland of the Hachimantai plateau (altitude, roughly 5,000 feet) are found forests, marshes, and ponds. In winter hoarfrosts silver the trees, but in early summer the fields are a pageant of flowers. I took this photograph in May, after boarding a lift near the Matsuo Mines and riding up to this spot. Snow still covered the ground, but actually spring was just around the corner.

17. OZE LILIES, NIKKO. The highland region called Oze, including the Ozegahara plain and the Ozenuma marsh, is part of Nikko National Park and stretches over four prefectures—Gumma, Fukushima, Niigata, and Tochigi. Surrounded by high mountains, Oze in the spring and summer is a treasure house of brilliant blossoms. Among the most charming are the water lilies, which gleam golden against the blue-black marsh waters.

18. RED BERRIES AT YUNOKO LAKE, NIKKO. The trees around the shore of the lake turn red and drop their leaves earlier than those on the mountainside. The variety and richness of scarlet and yellow larch groves make autumn the most wonderful season at Inner Nikko, especially when the sky is pure blue over the Senjogahara plain. The red berries of a plant with which I am not familiar contrast handsomely with the green water of the lake.

19. EZO REEDS, NIKKO. A volcanic eruption formed the Ozenuma marsh above the Ozegahara plain. The marsh has a circumference of less than 4 miles, but it is rich in water plants such as these fresh, green Ezo reeds. However, the marsh is apparently drying up and may someday be only a wet field.

20. PAMPAS FIELDS OF SENGOKUBARA, FUJI-HAKONE-IZU. The Sengokubara plain is surrounded by an outer ring of mountains running from Nagao Pass to Mount Kintoki and by an inner series of crater mountains including Mount Kozuka. Private villas and inns inject a jarring note of artificiality into what was once an unbroken plain of Japanese pampas, but the slope on the Nagao Pass side retains its pristine charm.

21. GILDED AUTUMN AT YUNOKO LAKE, NIKKO. The lake, which is 4,920 feet above sea level, measures less than 2 miles around and 40 feet in depth. Located about 7 miles north of Nikko, it is believed to have been formed when lava flow blocked the course of the Yukawa River. This picture shows the gleaming larches on the shore of the lake, which, as its name suggests (*yunoko*, "hot-water lake"), is fed by hot springs.

22. RED FUJI, FUJI-HAKONE-IZU. North of the main highway on the Fuji-Yoshida side of Lake Yamanaka is a small village with thatched roofs that seems to have been forgotten by time. It is said that the land on which the village stands was once beneath the surface of the lake. The area is a cameraman's paradise since it affords endless opportunities to photograph Fuji, either with the village in the foreground or alone in its majesty as in this picture.

23. NEW SNOW ON MOUNT DAISEN, DAISEN-OKI. Mount Daisen is not only the highest mountain in the Chugoku District, but also one of the most handsome. A fine highway leads all the way to the temple and village of Daisenji midway up the slope. The beech grove on the side of the mountain was especially lovely the day I photographed it. All the branches were bare, and a light snow had just fallen.

24. PEAKS AT DAWN, CHUBU MOUNTAINS. About ten days before a trip to photograph Oyama, I suffered an attack of gallstones, but on the scheduled day of departure I was in good shape and went according to plan. I spent the night in a small hut and on the following morning went to photograph the first light on the mountaintop. That is where the pain began again and continued for three days. The photograph shows the dawn of that third day, when I at last found relief from suffering.

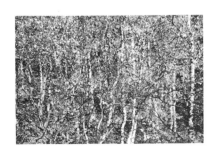

25. WHITE BIRCHES IN AUTUMN FOLIAGE, JOSHINETSU HEIGHTS. That part of the Johinetsu Park known as Shiga Heights is famous for its beautiful lakes and grassy plains as well as for fine stands of birch and an eternally blue sky. In October, as one follows the twisting road leading up the mountainside, the birch trees spread above like a golden canopy.

26. ALPINE FLOWERS, CHUBU MOUNTAINS. The gentle slope leading to the Goshikigahara highlands is famous as a wildflower paradise, but when I visited in August, the flowers were almost gone. When I asked an old woman about this, she replied: "The lives of flowers are brief." Perhaps unconsciously, she was quoting a two-line poem by Fumiko Hayashi; its concluding line is: "Only sorrow is in abundance."

27. AUTUMN SEASCAPE, SANIN COAST. Mention of the Sanin Coast usually evokes images of leaden-colored waters, but during the few bright, clear days of late autumn the ocean is a vibrant indigo. The splendor of the color quickly passes, however, as the snow-laden clouds of winter sweep across the sky.

28. SPRING HILLSIDE, SETO INLAND SEA. In spring the sloping hillsides of many of the islands in the Seto Inland Sea are decorated in a mosaic pattern of alternating fields of white, blooming vermifuge chrysanthemums and early wheat. The chrysanthemums, which blossom between May 15 and 20, are being cultivated in smaller and smaller quantities each year.

29. PEACH BLOSSOMS, SETO INLAND SEA. Taken earlier than the previous picture, this photograph shows fresh green wheat and delicate pink peach blossoms which bloom in March and April. Here in the vicinity of Onomichi a new bridge has recently been built to connect the mainland with a nearby island, but most people still prefer to cross from shore to shore in boats.

30. CHRYSANTHEMUMS, SETO INLAND SEA. The island of Manabe, located to the west of the Shiaku Islands, is—like the other islands in the Inland Sea—warm enough in winter to produce abundant crops of winter chrysanthemums, marigolds, and freesias. These flowers find ready markets, especially just before Christmas, in Osaka and Kobe.

31. SUNSET OVER ISLANDS, SETO INLAND SEA. I always think of the Seto Inland Sea as a place abounding in photogenic features that attract the admiration of people and provide safe havens for all kinds of sea life. Autumn there is especially beautiful when the sun sinks in the west and tints the sky first yellow, then orange, and finally madder-red.

32. WILD RHODODENDRON, ASO. Highways lead from Beppu to the mountains and from there to Aso, but to reach the areas where the *miyama-kirishima (Rhododendron kiusianum)* grow, one must climb on foot for a short distance. Fortunately, however, lodging is available at the Hokein Hot Springs. For a time insects had seriously damaged the plants, but they have recovered and now bloom as luxuriantly as in the past.

33. SEA GROTTO OF NANATSU-GAMA, GENKAI REGIONAL PARK (northwest coast of Kyushu). The name Nanatsu-gama, "seven pots," given to this section of the Dokizaki cape near Kyushu's Karatsu, is derived from the seven deeply water-worn grottoes in the rough, ribbed stone faces of the cliffs. It is possible to visit these caves in small boats and to thrill to the enchanting loveliness of the crystalline waters and the emerald aquatic plants clearly visible on the sea floor.

34. KISHUKU VILLAGE, SAIKAI. On the northwest coast of Fukue Island, one of the Goto group, is the village of Kishuku, an impressive sight with its white church steeple against the deep blue sea. Apparently Kishuku, like Hirado and Amakusa, was one of the places where Japan's last remaining Christians carried on covert religious observances after the government outlawed Christianity in the early seventeenth century. This photo was taken on a hot summer day.

35. FROZEN SEA, SHIRETOKO. During the severe winters of the Shiretoko Peninsula, ice floes build up and knife-edge winds from the Sea of Okhotsk freeze the seascape for as far as the eye can see. Only here and there do black boulders project through the frozen surface. This photo shows the offing in the vicinity of Utoro, midway up the northwest coast of the Shiretoko Peninsula.

36. BROKEN ICE FLOES, SHIRETOKO. During February and March, ice floes ram and crumple each other to produce grotesque vistas of this kind. The frozen seascape is most beautiful at either sunset or sunrise. Visiting in March because I was told that that might be the only time during the cold season when the bus to Utoro could get through, I arose early one morning and was able to take some good pictures of the desolate, eerie wasteland of ice.

37. FOREST LAKE, AKAN. The sound of an ax has never been heard in Akan, one of the most beautiful and unspoiled forest and lake areas on Hokkaido. Lake Onne, seen here as a gleaming, silver sheet, is located at the base of the so-called female Akan volcano. Since practically no one ever visits the region, its calm, pristine beauty remains undisturbed.

38. LAKE MASHU, AKAN. Mysterious Lake Mashu has no tributary rivers or streams, neither flowing into or out of it, and still its surface remains at a constant 1,152 feet above sea level. It is about 12 miles in circumference, and its waters are so pure that one can see down into their depths for over 100 feet. With a maximum depth of 700 feet, this is one of the deepest lakes in the world, second only to Russia's Lake Baikal. The islet in the middle of the lake is called Kamuinshu, "Residence of the Gods."

39. SNOW ON TOKACHI MOUNTAINS, DAISETSUZAN. Taken on the evening of the first clear day after several days of an early-March blizzard, this photo shows the extremely popular ski slope on the side of Mount Tokachi, located in the southwest corner of the park. Tokachi (6,815 ft.) is itself the main peak in a group which also includes mounts Biei, Oputateshike, and Chubetsu.

40. SWIRLING SNOW ON TOKACHI MOUNTAINS, DAISETSUZAN. I arose early and left my inn at Shirogane Hot Springs to climb Mount Tokachi for this photo. The temperature was several degrees below zero Fahrenheit, and the rice in our lunchboxes had frozen so hard that it crackled as we ate. After hurriedly taking some pictures, we began our return, but in departing I turned around to see the snow dust rising in wind-driven cloudlets from the white surface.

223

41. SNOW-CLAD TREES AT HAKKODA, TOWADA-HACHIMANTAI. Waiting out a heavy snowstorm, I shut myself in a mountain hut through day after day of blizzard. Finally, thinking the time was right and deciding to start out on a climb, I paused to take a few pictures before departure. I was fortunate to have a split second in which I could actually tell where the sun was. The lull in the storm, however, was barely long enough for me to click the shutter of my camera.

42. MOUNTAIN RAPIDS AT OIRASE, TOWADA-HACHIMANTAI. Twisting streams flowing from Lake Towada drop in waterfall veils at some places and at others race in rapids around blackened boulders flecked with golden leaves. The forest paths follow the course of the streams so closely that it is almost always possible to touch the water. The general mood is one of intimacy similar to that in the miniature gardens Japanese people have long admired.

43. REFLECTIONS IN AKANUMA MARSH, TOWADA-HACHIMANTAI. The single inn and shop at Tsuta Hot Springs still preserve their solitude. The marshes in the vicinity are all out-of-the-way and serenely undisturbed by passing time, but Akanuma marsh is probably more so than any other. Had I not enjoyed the guide services of Mr. Ogasawara, owner of the shop, I might not have been able to find my way to this secluded place.

44. AUTUMN LIGHT AT OIRASE, TOWADA-HACHIMANTAI. This mountain stream, dropping 634 feet at a very slight incline, is rich in varying scenery, with oaks, Judas trees, and maples intensifying its beauty. The stream is especially lovely when the leaves flame into colors about October 20, and about ten days later the reds and golds move from the mountains to the lower hills.

45. TWILIGHT OVER OZE MARSH, NIKKO. Located at an elevation of 5,463 feet, the Oze Marsh is similar in nature to those in arctic zones. Measuring about a mile from east to west and less than a mile north to south, this marsh has a maximum depth of 28 feet. In June, when the snows melt, one can see such scenes as this, when the fading sun sinks behind the mountain and the curtain of night falls silently.

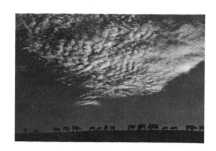

46. PASTURELAND AT DUSK, JOSHINETSU HEIGHTS. Autumn has come to the Shiga Heights. The leaves of the birch trees have fallen, the grasses have turned russet, and grazing cows hunt for a few last blades of grass under a vaulting sky hung with clouds gold and pink with the fading light. Tomorrow the weather will probably change. The Shiga Heights are a place of true rest for those of us whose lives are impoverished by urban environments.

47. RAINBOW AT KEGON FALLS, NIKKO. Plummeting 316 feet from Lake Chuzenji, Kegon Falls cascades in veils of frothing, emerald water which catches the sunlight to build a radiant rainbow bridge. The falls are 33 feet wide and the pit at the base is 66 feet deep. Smaller bead-curtain falls accentuate the grandeur of the white sheet which plummets in a sheer drop from lake level.

48. MOUNTAIN HOUSE, HAKUSAN. Habitable land is scarce in Hakusan, and forestry is the primary occupation. Consequently, in the past it was frequently impossible for newly married couples to set up their own household in a separate residence; and the resulting large families needed big houses built in the traditional, steep-roofed *gassho* style. Today new houses in modern styles may have spelled the doom of the rustically handsome old homes.

49. LIGHTHOUSE, HINOMISAKI CAPE (southwest coast of Kii Peninsula). This lighthouse, standing on a hill 650 feet high at the end of the cape, commands a splendid view of the sea. The sun shining directly on the surface of the water is strongly reminiscent of southern lands. The original lighthouse, built in 1895, was destroyed in World War II; the present one, constructed in 1951, has a strong beam that can be seen 28 miles out at sea.

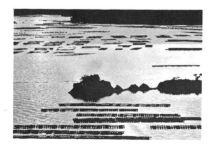

50. PEARL RAFTS, ISE-SHIMA. Over sixty years ago in this area, Kokichi Mikimoto and other pioneers were the first to produce cultured pearls on a large scale. Rafts, bearing suspended baskets of pearl oysters, lie sheltered from cold and storm in the calm waters of Ago Bay. The deeply indented and complicated topography of the bay is ideal for pearl culture, although today similar operations are in progress in other parts of the country.

51. MUSHIMA LIGHTHOUSE, SETO INLAND SEA. A total of 3,000 rock and reef outcroppings, including 600 full-scale islands, dot the waters of the Seto Inland Sea, which measures 273 miles in length and from 4 to 40 miles north in width. There are many lighthouses to guide ships among these islands. This one in the western part of Okayama Prefecture lights the straits between Mushima island and Misaki cape on the large island of Shikoku. Numerous seagoing vessels pass this way.

52. SHIONOMISAKI REEF BY DAY, YOSHINO-KUMANO. Shiono-misaki cape, the southernmost point of Honshu, juts out from the Kii Peninsula. An expanse of level land tops the rough, weathered cliffs falling steeply to the ocean about 260 feet below. Countless boulders and reefs rising from the water suggest a graveyard of stones; and when the sea is rough, turbulent waves crash mercilessly over the tops of the boulders.

53. SHIONOMISAKI REEF BY NIGHT, YOSHINO-KUMANO. As fading daylight turns the sky first lavender and then indigo, the Shionomisaki lighthouse brightens like a star to guide ships at sea. The light can be seen from as far away as 19.5 nautical miles. Standing at one side of the cape in order to take this photograph, I felt I could have stayed there forever thrilling to the mystic serenity of the scene.

54. LIGHTNING OVER BISAN SETO, SETO INLAND SEA. That part of the Inland Sea known as Bisan Seto is located at the busy straits where ferry service connects Honshu with Shikoku, running from Uno in Okayama Prefecture to Takamatsu in Kagawa Prefecture. The ferry boats plow the waters day and night, creating much bustle in the straits. When I took this night photo from an island in the sea, lightning in the mountains beyond the town of Tamano foretold impending rain.

55. ISLANDS OF MIZUSHIMA-NADA, SETO INLAND SEA. Islands sleeping on gilded waters in the last light of the setting sun contrast sharply with the industrial belt rapidly developing not far from the Mizushima district, near the famous old town of Kurashiki.

56. SEA WITH BOATS, SETO INLAND SEA. The 30-odd islands of the Shiaku group dot the silvery waters in the vicinity of Mount Washu on the Kojima Peninsula. In the distant past, this area was a departure point for expeditions against Korea, and even today the sailors on many ships bound for more distant lands come from this region. Seen from the north, the sea always glitters as it does in this photo.

57. ISLETS OF SOUTHERN KUJUKUTO, SAIKAI. The Kujukuto islets (literally, the "ninety-nine islands") dot the coastal sea for over 15 miles from Sasebo to Hirado and are divided into northern and southern groups. The waters around Kyushu are called the Western Sea, and true to their name, they offer dazzling spectacles of the sun setting in the west and working magical color transformations on the watery surface.

58. WAVES OF MOUNTAINS, SAIKAI. This photo indicates the breadth of view available from observation points in Sasebo. The ranges of island mountains look like series of waves rolling in, and on clear days, still other islands of the Goto group are visible in the distance.

59. SILVER SEA AT CAPE MUROTO, MUROTO-ANAN COAST REGIONAL PARK (southeastern coast of Shikoku). This photo shows the sea in a mood unusual for this part of the Shikoku coast. Ordinarily monstrous waves crash ceaselessly into the age-old boulders. The region is an infamous typhoon zone, and once, during an especially violent storm, the winds blew so hard that they broke the local anemometers. The cape offers an expansive view of the Pacific.

60. OUTSIDE TOMIOKA BAY, UNZEN-AMAKUSA. On the inner side of a small peninsula jutting out from the northwest corner of Amakusa Shimo Island, a long beach surrounds Tomioka Bay. On a hill on the peninsula are the remains of an old castle, which were covered with early summer grass when I visited to take this photograph of the waves washing the stones below.

61. HYUGA SEASCAPE, NICHINAN COAST REGIONAL PARK (southeastern coast of Kyushu). Even on calm days the Pacific waves roughly beat the stones on the shore of this palm-dotted area. The picture shows the silvery white of the rising sun reflected on the water.

62. AMAKUSA SEASCAPE, UNZEN-AMAKUSA. Quiet dawn clouds over unruffled waters and misty islands characterize the inner section of the Amakusa district. The outer area, though, is constantly buffeted by the harsh winds and waves of the East China Sea.

63. HAMLET AT TAKACHIHO, KIRISHIMA-YAKU. Peace and the golden light of autumn gently envelop a small village which seems steeped in myths of the descent from heaven of the gods who were traditionally believed to have given birth to the Japanese people. The boulders and cliffs, wonderfully weathered in almost vertical patterns, are a striking sight. The village is near the headwaters of the Gokase River and the famous Takachiho Gorge.

64. MOUNT KAIMON BY NIGHT, KIRISHIMA-YAKU. Mount Kaimon stands guard over the entrance to Kagoshima Bay, at the southern end of the Satsuma Peninsula. In spring when the rape flowers bloom, its base turns yellow green, a sharp contrast to the black volcanic sand gently washed by Pacific waves. At night the softly rounded shape of the mountain is ornamented with a few jewel-like lights gleaming from isolated houses.

65. CORAL SHALLOWS, OKINOERABU ISLAND (between Kyushu and Okinawa). Transparent gold wavelets lap gently at the pearly coral sands of the beaches of Okinoerabu, a small island just north of Okinawa. Coral reefs girdle the entire island.

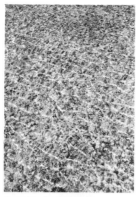

66. RIPPLES OVER CORAL, OKINOERABU ISLAND (same as above). Sunlight scattered by gentle breezes flashes like dissolved jewels over the coral not far beneath the surface. The crystalline water here is clean, warm, and unpolluted by the industrial wastes of the main islands.

67. CLIFFS ON SAGA ISLAND, SAIKAI. Located in the Goto Archipelago stretching off the northwest coast of Kyushu, Saga Island seems lonely in the East China Sea. Formed by volcanic eruptions, its volcanic materials have become exposed as the topsoil has been eroded. The island is consequently of great scientific importance.

68. SNOW ON SHIRETOKO MOUNTAINS, SHIRETOKO. Remotely situated on a horn-shaped peninsula jutting into the Sea of Okhotsk, the forbidding Shiretoko Mountains, locked all winter in ice and snow, were long considered the *ultima Thule* of Japan. A small colony is located on the shores of Utoro halfway up the peninsula, but few people venture very far into the wilderness. This photograph of the Shiretoko main peaks was taken from the air in June.

69. ICE FLOES, SHIRETOKO. Throughout the bitter Shiretoko winter, huge masses of ice pile up on one another as they rumble inland from the Sea of Okhotsk. Even in the day, when the sun plays dazzling light tricks on the ice mounds, the temperature remains well below freezing, and fish, which freeze immediately upon being removed from the water, must be thawed in boiling water before they can be eaten raw (as is the Japanese custom).

70. EARLY SPRING IN HACHIMAN MARSH, TOWADA-HACHIMAN-TAI. Spring comes late in the undulating plain and marsh at Hachimantai, but in May the ice begins to thaw and snow finally starts melting. Then cobalt water and lingering stripes of white snow combine in dramatically beautiful patterns. After the snow has melted, a riot of wildflowers and other alpine flora burst into bloom.

229

71. HOT SPRING AT GOSHOGAKE, TOWADA-HACHIMANTAI. Although Japan's many hot-spring resorts are gradually modernizing and assuming an atmosphere of luxurious comfort, Goshogake Hot Springs, in the northwestern section of Hachimantai on the Akita Prefecture side, remains simple and old-fashioned. The hot-mud eruptions in the marsh are grotesque and awe-inspiring.

72. KITAYAMAZAKI SHORELINE, RIKUCHU COAST. Miyako is the center of the Rikuchu Coast National Park. South of this city, the coastline is submerged and richly indented; to the north, the shore is rugged and rolling with handsomely eroded caves, tunnels, and great boulders. This photo shows Kitayamazaki, considerably north of Miyako, at a spot where awesome, naturally weathered stone formations brave the pounding ocean waves.

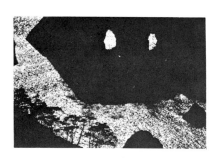

73. NATURAL TUNNELS, RIKUCHU COAST. Tens of thousands of years of battles between cliffs and sea have produced the magnificent stone grotesqueries of the Kitayamazaki coast, known as the most spectacular of Japan's several dramatically eroded shorelines. The two tunnels here were photographed from the cliff on the Kitayamazaki Peninsula.

74. MOUNTAINS ON MOUNTAINS, TOWADA-HACHIMANTAI. Of all the mountainous regions in this country, Northeast Honshu, where Towada-Hachimantai is located, has perhaps the most rugged mountain terrain. Here, instead of stunning, isolated peaks, one range follows another in a continuous pattern. These mountains were photographed from an airplane in early winter.

75. SNOW SLOPE, TOWADA-HACHIMANTAI. This sweeping expanse, an excellent skiing spot, rises at a regular incline from Toshichi Hot Springs to the top of the mountain. At Toshichi, skiers and mountain climbers can warm themselves for the ascent or, while sipping the local sakè, enjoy the color and fading light of day reflected in the splendor of the surrounding scenery.

76. DEAD TREES IN SNOW, JOSHINETSU HEIGHTS. After a day of climbing in the Kusatsu-Shirane area, my eyes happened to light on these stark, black trees half buried in heaped snow and casting skeletal shadows on the gleaming white. They seemed a beautiful example of natural art. Later I climbed to the crater lake called Yugama, where ice formations presented another example of nature in a similarly artistic mood.

77. SNOW PANORAMA AT KASAGADAKE, JOSHINETSU HEIGHTS. Northwest of Kusatsu Hot Springs, no footprints spoil the placid perfection of the snow, but rows of blackened trees weave harmonious patterns across the whiteness. In the middle ground of the photo is Kasagadake, one of the most famous peaks in the Shiga Heights, and in the background are the Togakushi Mountains, which can rarely be seen from this great a distance.

78. SNOWSCAPE AT MOUNT GOZEN, HAKUSAN. Mount Gozen is the tallest of the three main peaks of the Hakusan Range, located partly in Ishikawa and partly in Gifu prefectures. Hakusan ("white mountain"), which some say is named for the eternal veil of white clouds around the tops of the peaks, is the site of the Shiroyamahime Shrine. The snow on Mount Gozen rarely melts, even in summer.

79. SNOWY GROVE, JOSHINETSU HEIGHTS. I visited the Togakushi highlands in May when cherry blossoms had already fallen in the lowlands, but in the mountains a blanket of snow still covered the ground among the birches and occasional groves of various other trees, whose branch tracery and green lichen attracted me greatly.

80. WINTER AT SENGATAKI FALLS, CHICHIBU-TAMA. The Arakawa river, which originates on Mount Kimpu, passes the outskirts of the city of Kofu and then flows through deeply eroded gorges of the Shosen Ravine. Farther on, as the Fuji River, it flows past imposing boulders and finally to the Pacific Ocean. Above Kofu, about two miles from the Tenjin Forest, are located the Sengataki waterfalls. In winter the water is almost as icy as the snow which remains for months on surrounding rocks.

81. HAMASAKA DUNES, SANIN COAST. Indigo sea and orange-tinted sands contrast strikingly at the Hamasaka Dunes, located outside the city of Tottori. These sand hills, unusually extensive for Japan, are thought to be formed by sea winds whipping up sands transported to the vicinity by the Sendai River.

82. DUNES AND SNOW, SANIN COAST. The snow clouds of the leaden winter skies on the Japan Sea coast drift landward until, stopped by a barrier of mountains, they deposit most of their snow on the hills. Although little falls on the dunes themselves, they are sometimes covered to the extent shown in this dramatic buff and white composition. Children ski on the snow-covered dune slopes.

83. ISLANDS AT BISAN SETO, SETO INLAND SEA. Smoke from copper refineries killed the verdure on the more than 30 islands in this area, leaving them bald and naked. Recently, however, a method has been devised to render the fumes harmless by extracting the sulfuric acid; as a result, greenery is returning. Ferries connect the islands with Uno in Okayama Prefecture on the mainland.

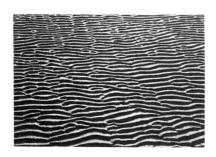

84. BEACH PATTERNS, SETO INLAND SEA. Near this handsomely engraved Shinmaiko Beach are a few inns serving outstanding seafood where guests can enjoy the calm pleasure of the placid Seto Inland Sea.

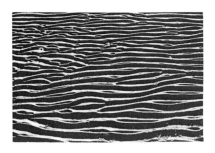

85. SAME. At maximum low tides, which usually occur three days after the new and three days after the full moon, the patterns etched in the sand by retreating waves and influenced by the direction of the wind take the form of horizontal stripes, vertical stripes, or netlike patterns.

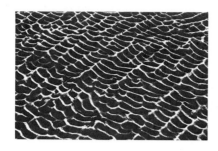

86. SAME. Dusk, especially in autumn, is the loveliest time at the Inland Sea, for then the sun gilds the beach and slowly turns it to rosy gold. Later the white light of the moon turns the sand silver, and flame lures of night fishermen twinkle on the waves.

87. SAME. The lines and footprints left by birds and small creatures in the sand are pleasant to investigate. But in recent years the Inland Sea has become a favorite summer playground, while in winter cultivators and reapers of edible seaweeds disturb the tranquillity. Unfortunately, it is no longer possible to appreciate fully the wonder of the patterns carved in the beach.

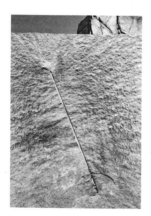

88. STONE QUARRY, SETO INLAND SEA. For many centuries stone has been quarried from the islands of the Inland Sea; in fact, the foundations of Osaka Castle and many other much older buildings were constructed of materials from the area. Of course, in the past quarry workers used only hammer and chisel, but today compressed-air drills and cutting equipment have vastly speeded up the process.

89. FIELD OF ERODED LIMESTONE, AKIYOSHIDAI REGIONAL PARK (western Honshu near Yamaguchi City). Akiyoshi Plateau is composed largely of limestone, which wind and rain have weathered into strange tombstone shapes. Beneath the earth nearby are numerous vertical and horizontal caves which give the region the forbidding name of Hell Valley.

90. SEA-CARVED ROCK, NICHINAN COAST REGIONAL PARK (southeastern coast of Kyushu). Many centuries of Pacific Ocean wind and waves have worn this rocky shore into weird shapes. Moonlit views of this kind can be observed from a clifftop where there is a garden of cactus plants.

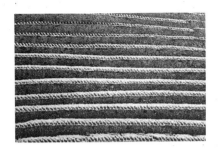

91. STAIRSTEP WHEAT FIELD, SETO INLAND SEA. Agricultural land is so needed in Japan that terracing must be used in order to farm even the steepest hillsides. Farmers of the Inland Sea as well as the mainland use this method. The fresh greenery peeping over the stone retaining walls is wheat, already green in February.

92. FISHING FLEET, SETO INLAND SEA. Though winter winds sometimes churn up triangular whitecaps on the surface of the Inland Sea, they suddenly cease in the springtime, and calm waters once again glitter opalescent under the sun. When this happens, the fishermen put out to sea in hope of rich catches. April and May, when the fish are most abundant, are called the "islands of fish" months.

93. BEECH TREES IN SNOW, DAISEN-OKI. Daisen, called the only true mountain in the Chugoku District, is an extremely popular climbing and skiing area for people from Osaka, Kobe, and Kyushu. A newly completed highway provides easy access, and the village of Daisenji, midway up the slope, offers lodging. In winter the area rests under deep snows.

94. NATURAL BRIDGE AT KUNIGA, DAISEN-OKI. When seen on a map, the Oki Archipelago, located about 30 miles north of the Shimane Peninsula, seems to be one large island; but in fact, there are more than 180 islets. The immense tunnels and caves in the towering rock, some of them almost 1,000 feet high, bear clear witness to the power of wind and waves. On calm days, boats take tourists to sea for better views of these magnificent natural structures.

95. DEAD CORAL, OKINOERABU ISLAND (between Kyushu and Okinawa). When alive, coral animals, seen from small boats sailing within the great reef encircling the island, seem a virtual flower garden of red, blue, green, and purple; but sooner or later they die, turn pallid gray, and wash up on stones on the shore.

234

96. SUN OVER SNOW, SHIRETOKO. Late in the afternoon of a cloudless day in March near the ice floes in the vicinity of Utoro, I spied this huge boulder, sturdy enough to withstand the worst Siberian cold and howling winds, with a brilliant blaze of late sunlight accenting its mass.

97. NARUTO CURRENT, SETO INLAND SEA. The rapid Naruto Current flows in swirls and whirlpools between Awaji Island and the city of Naruto on Shikoku. It has long been a famous tourist attraction. During the spring tides, the current moves at even higher speeds, sometimes reaching 12 knots. The larger whirlpools have diameters ranging from 50 to 100 feet and are a grave peril to ships approaching them.

98. SAME. Although the popular way to view the whirlpools is by boat from the Shikoku side, I think it is better to observe them from the cliffs of Awaji Island. My vantage point in this case was a narrow precipice at Tozaki, where it is possible to see the swirling waters at close range and marvel at the violence of nature's energy.

99. SUNSET, SETO INLAND SEA. The sun setting over the sea in this spring scene is beautiful, but so are sunsets in any season. The change in the sun from flaming incandescence to rich gold and the resulting transformation in the colors of the sky from blue to orange, red, purple, and finally indigo are incomparable. The pattern of horizontals in this scene creates a mood of indescribable calm.

100. WALLS of ASO CRATER, ASO. After a number of trips to Aso, I became acquainted with one of the men who guide tourists to the crater on horseback and who sometimes must haul out of the smoking hole visitors who fall in. Once I took a trip with this man into the crater itself. As we descended, with the burning rocks and belching fumes all around us, the heat gradually penetrated the thick soles of our mountain-climbing shoes. It seemed we had entered an unworldly phantasmagoria.

101. SMOKE FROM MOUNT TOKACHI, DAISETSUZAN. The Taisho crater of Mount Tokachi, located in the southwest extremity of the park, first erupted on May 24, 1926. At that time, rushing lava and hot mud from the newly formed crater filled two local rivers, and 144 people lost their lives. Photo taken in March.

102. SAME. When I set out from my inn at Shirogane Hot Springs on a clear March day, it was the first time I had tried mountain climbing since reaching middle age, and it was also the first time I had ever seen snow of such a beautiful texture. I had intended to ascend the mountain fairly quickly, but I became absorbed in taking pictures along the way, and it was noon before I reached the top, where heaps of newly fallen snow lay among the rising pillars of smoke from the crater.

103. NEW MOUNT SHOWA, SHIKOTSU-TOYA. On December 20, 1943, the land at the base of Mount Usu near Lake Toya rumbled and shook severely. Gradually the level of the land rose and eruptions occurred until, by 1945, what had been rice fields was a small mountain. It was named in honor of the present Showa reign period. The postmaster of a nearby town owned the land and was able to watch it being transformed into a volcano, which now belongs to him.

104. SAKURAJIMA'S MAIN CRATER, KIRISHIMA-YAKU. Sakurajima is an island formed by volcanic action in Kinko Bay. In recent times it has erupted with disastrous results on several occasions. In 1914, lava covered eight villages; and the eruption of 1946 dumped sufficient debris into the bay to form a bridge connecting the island with the nearby Osumi Peninsula, and lava covered two more villages. The photograph shows (left to right) the north peak, middle peak, and the still active south peak.

105. THE FEMALE AKAN VOLCANO, AKAN. Two volcanoes, called male and female, face each other across Lake Akan. The female, almost 5,000 feet high, has hot spring resorts on its slopes, and to ascend it requires about two hours of brisk walking. At the mouth of the crater there is a spot where the smoking heart of the mountain can be seen directly below. In the photo, Lake Akan is in the middle ground and the Akan range of mountains is in the distance.

236

106. AKAN FUJI, AKAN. Circling the crater of the female Akan volcano and moving beyond the point from which Lake Akan is visible, the traveler suddenly sees the lovely black shape of Akan Fuji. My photo gains impact because of the sea of white clouds below its graceful peak. The pillar of smoke in the foreground rises from the female Akan volcano.

107. SAME. Akan Fuji is a subsidiary peak related to the female Akan, smoke from which is seen rising at the left. In front of the Akan Fuji volcano, some crater lakes already in the process of formation give clear indication of the way volcanic regions develop. After a full day of taking pictures of the female Akan, I returned to my inn and found everyone was out searching for me. It seems several bears had been seen in the neighborhood the day before.

108. NIGHT SKY OVER MOUNT HODAKA, CHUBU MOUNTAINS. Early spring comes to the highlands in May when the birch trees bud. Since there are so many sightseers bustling about in the daytime, I decided to take my pictures at night. The moon was shining brightly when I arrived to photograph this scene, and the sky was filled with innumerable stars. The snow gleamed pale in the moonlight.

109. MOUNT ASO CRATER, ASO. We are told that in the distant past, towering Mount Aso dominated the landscape of Kyushu. If so, it must have been much grander than it is now, and even today its outer ring measures almost 13 miles in diameter. After numerous eruptions, it probably became unable to support its own weight and crumbled. Eruptions in the center of the original crater created what is today called Mount Aso. Of its five craters, only the main one, Nakadake, remains active.

110. EXTINCT CRATER, ASO. Of the complicated volcanic system that makes up Mount Aso, four craters are extinct and one is active. This inactive crater, Mount Neko, blew its top off entirely and then lapsed into silence. The photograph underscores the fearsome might of a natural world in which so great a power as a volcano can die and undergo erosion.

111. MOUNT NEKO BY NIGHT, ASO. The sharp teeth of the crater's top ridge bear witness to the furor of the internal raging that blew off the mountain's top. The Aso area is very beautiful at night, when clumps of red rock can be seen flaming in the still active central crater. But thousands of people visit the area yearly, and the congestion is usually oppressive.

112. KANNON GORGE, SOUTHERN ALPS. Although it was late April, the dead of winter still reigned at Kannon Gorge, and its stone walls were covered with ice and snow. Using tire chains to prevent slippage on the snowy roads, I finally managed to force my rented car up to Yashajin Pass. From this vantage point most of the important mountains of the Southern Alps group are visible.

113. RAPIDS AT OIRASE, TOWADA-HACHIMANTAI. Today automobiles can pass by here so easily that almost no one appreciates the profound beauty of the region's harmonious combination of calm and action. In this scene the tranquilly resting maple leaves contrast beautifully with the headlong rush of the rapids. This is a place which deserves the careful attention of a traveler on foot.

114. KEGON FALLS, NIKKO. If I divided the scenery of Nikko into the active and the calm, Kegon Falls would be the epitome of activity. The central white plume of water drops 330 feet, and halfway down there is a curtain of small subsidiary waterfalls. In autumn, reflecting the reds and golds of flaming foliage, the water takes on new beauty. I suspect that no country in the world has more waterfalls than Japan, and no people use them more in their art and gardening.

115. LATE AUTUMN AT LAKE CHUZENJI, NIKKO. I took a short walk on the shores of Lake Chuzenji a little off the beaten track in a place where no automobiles passed. A thick carpet of leaves covered the path and crackled hearteningly as I walked on them. Along the shore stood buildings belonging to the embassies of a number of countries, and it was pleasant to observe them symbolically conversing in the architectural accents of their lands.

238

116. SUNSET AT LAKE CHUZENJI, NIKKO. The sun was dropping slowly behind the mountains beyond the lake. The blue sky and water turned red. Like a network of blood vessels, the leafless branches of the trees seemed to fill the entire space overhead. There was no wind and the lake was very placid. Staying at a house on the shore of the lake, I went out into the perfect stillness of the starlit night and experienced a true dialogue with nature.

117. RYUZU FALLS, NIKKO. The topography of Nikko gives rise to a number of waterfalls. Among the most famous are Kegon, which I have already described; Kirifuri, which is divided into several stages; Urami, which is said to be more beautiful when viewed from behind the falling water; and Ryuzu, which races like rapids over a stone bed.

118. EARLY MORNING, CHUBU MOUNTAINS. In order to reach the top of Oyama in time for the sunrise, I had to get up at four in the morning and climb a very steep incline. Although I procured the services of a young man to carry my equipment, I was tired by the time we reached the summit at 5:30 because I am not a very good climber. Unfortunately, the sunrise itself was invisible, but the mountains of the Ushiro-Takeyama range were nonetheless beautiful in the early mists.

119. MOON OVER SHORE, KIRISHIMA-YAKU. Yaku Island is the southernmost area in Japan's national park system. Its mountains are higher than those on Kyushu. The local people say it rains here 366 days a year. Many of the island's cedar trees are over a thousand years old. On my visit to Yaku I stayed at a house by the beach. The evening of the day I arrived, I opened my door to find a full moon gracing the eastern part of a sky from which the last light of day had not yet vanished.

ABOUT THE AUTHORS

YOICHI MIDORIKAWA is one of Japan's foremost photographers, specializing in nature photography. He makes his home in Okayama City, near the shores of the Inland Sea. His published work includes *Japon Japonais* (published in Switzerland), *Yoroppa no fukei* (European Scenery), *Seto Naikai* (Seto Inland Sea), and *Kokuritsu koen* (National Parks of Japan). He is a director of the Japan Photographers' Society and a member of the Photographic Society of Japan and has received numerous prestigious Japanese awards for his photography.

JIRO OSARAGI is one of Japan's most highly regarded novelists, with over twenty-five books to his credit. Several of his novels have been translated into English, including *Homecoming* and *The Journey*. He is a member of the Japanese Academy of Arts and a recipient of the Japanese Order of Cultural Merit.

MAGOICHI KUSHIDA is a well-known poet and essayist. His published work includes eight volumes of essays, six volumes of belles-lettres, several volumes of poetry, and numerous books and articles on Japanese nature and scenic beauty. He formerly taught literature and ethics at the Tokyo University of Foreign Studies.

MICHIO OI is chief of the Planning Section, Department of National Parks, Japanese Ministry of Welfare. He also lectures on landscaping, conservation, and park beautification at Tokyo and Nihon universities.

WILLIAM O. DOUGLAS, Justice of the Supreme Court of the United States of America, is also well known as a nature lover and conservationist.

The "weathermark" identifies this book as having been planned and produced at the Tokyo offices of John Weatherhill, Inc., in collaboration with Tankosha, Kyoto. Book design and layout by Gan Hosoya. Typography by Meredith Weatherby. Composition by General Printing Company, Yokohama. Platemaking and printing by Nissha Printing Company, Kyoto. Bound at the Okamoto Binderies, Tokyo. Set in Monotype Perpetua, with hand-set Optima for display.